John William Shannon

A Memoir

ISBN 978-0-9956899-9-2

Published by
University of Winchester
Sparkford Road
Winchester
Hampshire SO22 4NR

Printed and bound by
Sarsen Press
22 Hyde Street
Winchester
Hampshire SO23 7DR

To my family and particularly to my wife
Eileen who was my strength

List of contents

List of Illustrations

A message from the Vice Chancellor of the University of Winchester

I have been eagerly awaiting John's memoirs ever since I first heard that he intended to write them.

John is a very special man. He has received the Prime Minister's Points of Life Award and a Harrogate and district volunteering Oscar, as well as being shortlisted for the Britain's Best Volunteer award. He has also been recognised by the Duchess of Cornwall as the Royal Voluntary Service's Diamond Champion. On top of this national recognition, he is dearly loved by everyone he encounters and has given so much to our local communities.

John is a staunch friend of the University and has continued to support us since he left King Alfred's College over 80 years ago. Last year John turned 100, and to celebrate his career and recognise his love of sport, the University of Winchester renamed our Multi Use Games Area in his honour. He has led an amazing and varied life, and his stories never fail to delight and enthral. I am so glad that he has chosen to commit his memories to paper.

I hope this book brings you – the reader – as much delight as John's stories have brought me over the years. We could all do with more people like John in our lives.

Joy Carter
Vice Chancellor
University of Winchester

Foreword

John William Shannon is a distinguished alumnus of the University of Winchester and, most importantly, an exemplar of the values on which it prides itself.[1] This memoir is his story and is a most welcome addition to the two histories published in 2015 during a year of celebration of the 175th anniversary of the University's foundation in 1840 as a Diocesan Training School (later College). 'Alumni Voices: The Changing Experience of Higher Education', an oral history of former students and staff covering the previous sixty years, was published in April.[2] November saw the publication of 'Winchester University: 175 Years of Higher Education', which updated in words and pictures, the history of the institution from its foundation.[3] As John achieved his centenary in 2016, his own history runs parallel with many of the major developments in the history of the university and the history of education more generally.

The memoir was brought to the attention of the Alumni Voices authors by one of the project participants, Stephen Baldwin, who attended John's centenary celebrations. We are very grateful to Stephen for recognising its value not only to John's family and friends for whom it was originally intended but also to a wider public, particularly those interested in the social history and the history of

---

[1] The University of Winchester is a values-driven institution. Its mission statement is, 'To educate, to advance knowledge and to serve the common good'. Its values accord with this mission.

[2] Stephanie Spencer, Andrea Jacobs, Camilla Leach, *Alumni Voices: The Changing Experience of Higher Education* (Winchester: University of Winchester Press, 2015).

[3] Tom Beaumont James, *Winchester University: 175 Years of Higher Education* (Third Millennium Press, 2015).

education in the twentieth century as well as the history of the Royal Navy in World War II.

While we received the memoir in written form, it was originally an oral history. We have been advised by John's daughter, Eileen, that the family wished to have something special to commemorate her father's 100th birthday. She wrote to us:

> About 18 months ago I asked my father to record some of his memories as I wanted to create 'something' for his 100th birthday. We started doing it after lunch on Sundays. Whenever Dad went down to stay with my brother in Cambridge, Dad would continue with his recordings. Eventually after about six months, Dad decided that he had recorded quite a few memories, probably, 'enough', as he put it. I was tempted to say that there would never be 'enough'. He can remember so much and in the most minute detail...

> ...So, the next problem was to arrange for the recordings to be written down. By asking around I discovered a very interesting lady who lives in Manchester. She came over to meet us and was enthralled with my dad, as is everyone! She said she would be honoured to do the work. Claire typed up all the recordings almost word for word and then sorted them into chapters. [4]

Regrettably, 'the something' that Eileen refers to in her e mail did not happen due to family illness and it was then that Stephen stepped in to ask if the university could assist in any way. As a result, the University of Winchester is delighted to support the publication of

---

[4] E mail from Eileen Pearson to Andrea Jacobs, dd. 9.11.2016.

the memoir. As one of the authors of Alumni Voices, I am privileged to have been asked to write a foreword. We were not involved with the original recordings but as Eileen has confirmed they were typed up almost verbatim, the comments which follow are based on the manuscript we received as a transcription of a series of oral interviews.[5]

The chapters his daughter Eileen refers to in her e mail form the main body of what follows. Some footnotes have been added where we think further explanations might be useful and where further information has subsequently been brought to our attention. After completing the recordings, John decided to write a little more especially about his wife, Eileen. These comments have been inserted into the text at relevant points. They appear in italics to distinguish them from the original oral memoir. Where they are footnoted, these are prefaced with an indication that John has advised us of this additional information separately.

Oral history is not an exact science and professional views on its use vary widely. It has its own extensive literature which it would not be appropriate to discuss here but suffice it to say that there is an optimistic camp and a pessimistic one. The optimists recognise the value of both bringing to the forefront the story of those whose stories might not otherwise be told and as Philip Gardner has recognised that: 'The story of a life may also become the story of the historical landscape within which the life has been lived'.[6] The view of

---

[5] There are disadvantages, but only for us in that we have not heard the original recordings nor did we have the opportunity to ask further questions which we might have done had we been actually interviewing John ourselves.

[6] Philip Gardner, 'Oral History in Education: Teacher's Memory and Teachers' History', *History of Education Journal* 32.2 2003:184

the pessimists is summarised again by Gardner, writing with Peter Cunningham: 'Such data draw upon the vagaries of individual memory; that they are the products of the present and not, as with the historical document, of the past.[7]

As historians of education who have employed oral history methodology in our work, we are, quite clearly, on the side of the optimists and this memoir demonstrates how disadvantages are outweighed by the benefits, particularly when the result reveals the story of such a rich life as John's played out against the background of the 20th and 21st centuries. At the outset, it seems important to point out that although the memoir is John's life story, it is also a love story. John met his wife Eileen when they were both in their teens and although she died on 14th November, 2008, she is still in John's thoughts every day. John's story is also Eileen's story.

John was born in 1916 and therefore grew up in the inter-war period which was turbulent both politically and in socio-economic terms. He did well at school, even though he went to more than one, and secured a scholarship to secondary school, a year earlier than was usual, at the age of 10. He did exceptionally well academically and in the field of sport. His secondary education provided him with a good education with the promise of a successful future. After leaving school and an interim year acting as a student teacher as, at 17, he was too young to go to college or university, John decided that he liked teaching and his future would be in education. He attended King Alfred's College for two years to obtain the necessary qualifications.

---

[7] Peter Cunningham and Philip Gardner, *Becoming Teachers: Texts and Testimonies 1907-1950* (London and Portland, Oregon: Woburn Press, 2004) 4-5.

John immediately obtained a post on leaving college but his career was interrupted by World War II where he served in the Royal Naval Volunteer Reserve. He entered the Royal Navy on 1st September 1939, joining HMS Dunvegan Castle as an Able Seaman, Captain's messenger and ship's schoolmaster, for the latter he was paid nine pence a day, a rate laid down by King Charles II. This ship was torpedoed three times and then lost. After officer training, he joined HMS Quentin Roosevelt, the first ship commissioned in the Royal Navy Section Belge in January 1941 as First Lieutenant. When this ship was decommissioned he left the Section Belge to be appointed to his own commands. At a comparatively young age, he subsequently commanded Royal Navy ships from 1942 until the cessation of hostilities, undertaking a number of special operations. He lost only one ship during that time. He had married Eileen in January 1941 and his two children were born during the war years.

After the war, he resumed his teaching career by returning to the same secondary school where he had been Head of PE before the war. By a very happy accident, he moved to a primary school in Halstead in Essex, where he was appointed headteacher. He achieved this first headship only nine years after leaving teacher training college, with his war service intervening. From Halstead, he moved to another headship at another primary school in Essex. As in his naval service, he was in the position of being senior to many people older than himself. In 1964, John decided that he needed a change of direction and became first a senior lecturer, then a principal lecturer and then Schools' Officer at the Margaret McMillan teacher training college in Bradford. He remained there until his retirement in 1975. During the latter part of this time, he was also the Chairman of Assessors for Leeds University and a member of the Board of Studies for Leeds University.

Retirement gave John the opportunity to continue his many hobbies, volunteering activities and to enjoy holidays abroad. John and Eileen were fortunate to have many happy years of retirement together. Unfortunately, in the 1990s Eileen began to experience symptoms of Alzheimer's disease. John supported her fight to keep them at bay as long as possible and helped to nurse her when it became necessary. Following her death in 2008, John has lived alone and is now living in a residential home in Harrogate, from choice rather than from necessity.

There are at least four recurring themes that are woven throughout John's story. The first and most significant is his love for his wife Eileen and his appreciation of her support for so many years of their lives together. The second theme concerns his volunteering activities which he has always undertaken from his teenage years when he became secretary of his local League of Nations Union. The awards he has garnered for his volunteering activities are numerous. His love of sport is the third theme. He has enjoyed sporting activities all his life and ensured that the children at his schools had opportunities to enjoy as many sports as possible. His most recent award relates to his lifelong service to football and was awarded by the Football Association. The final theme is that his life has been one of almost continuous learning from his own schooldays onwards. He undertook many courses during his career to improve his knowledge and qualifications and following his retirement he continued to study for pleasure.

Alongside his own autobiography, John also tells the story of his wife Eileen who was born in 1919 and had a rather unusual early life growing up in India before being sent back to England alone for her education. She met John when she was only 16. After leaving school she gained a prestigious appointment in the Civil Service but which she had to relinquish on her marriage to John. Against the backdrop of World War II, the early years of the marriage were hard, especially when Eileen moved, with her baby son to be near John in a remote part of Scotland. However, after the war she and John worked hard, prospered and were able to offer young John and Eileen a comfortable upbringing and good educations. Once they were grown she pursued her early ambition to teach which she did very successfully until she retired at the same time as John enjoying her retirement until the effects of Alzheimer's became too much.

In spite of the successes in his life, many of which have been publicly recognised, John writes of himself very modestly.[8] He does not emphasise his numerous achievements but rather brushes them aside as nothing special. He is much more comfortable praising other people and there are very few people whom he has encountered in his long life for whom he has a bad word. When John speaks of his days at King Alfred's College, he highlights, the camaraderie and community spirit that existed amongst these small close-knit groups, drawn together for a common purpose. His description echoes those of the alumni who took part in the Alumni Voices project, as are many of the memories he recalls. When he writes of the war, he does not glorify it. Instead he remembers all the good men he served with and more especially those who died. When speaking of his days as a headteacher, he applauds the staff who worked for him and the parents who were supportive of the schools. The most fervent of his

---

[8] John does not mention this in the memoir but we have been advised by his daughter that during David Cameron's premiership, John was one of his 'Points of Light', e mail from Eileen Pearson to Andrea Jacobs, 22.7.2017. Points of Light are described as being 'Outstanding individual volunteers-people who are making a change in their community. www.pointsoflight.gov.uk.

praise is reserved for his family, his children and grandchildren and especially for his wife Eileen to whom he attributes much of the success they enjoyed working together to achieve common goals.

Inevitably, there are fewer and fewer people alive who can directly relate to John and Eileen's story: few people who were born during or in the wake of World War I, to grow up and marry in World War II and build their lives together in the austere post-war years before enjoying the benefits of greater prosperity in later life. Although more people will be able to relate to the story of seeing a loved one suffer from Alzheimer's, for many readers, John and Eileen's story will be one that belongs to their parents or their grandparents rather than themselves. This is its great strength and value, becoming as it does not just the story of a life but the story of the historical landscape within which the life has been lived. In order to obviate any attempt to put a presentist interpretation on the events that John describes, we will contextualise just two areas where the historical landscape has changed considerably from that which John describes: the field of education and the role of women.

That John went to a secondary school is noteworthy. During his schooldays, a secondary education was for the few rather than the many. The majority of children left school at the age of 14 without formal qualifications. Educationally, the period may be viewed as one of consolidation and preparation. There were a lot of debates about lots of ideas. The government's Consultative Committee produced five reports between 1923 and 1933, with a further one in 1938. All these made recommendations that were not implemented until after the 1944 Education Act which was the first time that secondary education became available to all and the school leaving age was raised to 15.

Although some of John's later professional education did take place at university, his initial teacher training took place at a single sex teacher training college. He is at pains to state in the memoir that the qualifications to enter either were almost the same and one should not be regarded as inferior to the other. In the first part of the twentieth century, teacher training colleges were numerous and many, like King Alfred's College in Winchester, were controlled by the Church who had had a virtual monopoly of teacher training until Local Education Authorities were permitted to open secular colleges from 1902. Although many were absorbed into other institutions or developed their own role beyond, but often including teacher training, the majority had disappeared by the 1980s.

John emphasises in the memoir that the children at his schools experienced a very traditional style of education to ensure they achieved their potential. In the immediate post-war period, the implementation of the 1944 Education Act was paramount, providing as it did the first opportunity for all children to enjoy education at a secondary level. The grammar school was the aim of any bright child in the post-war years and therefore, as many as were able, were drilled to pass the 11+ examination. When the Conservative party gained power in 1951, lasting until 1964, they held firm in the belief that a selective system was the best way to bring forward talent even though in many parts of the world selective systems were being replaced with comprehensive ones. Other than a handful of trial schemes, comprehensive schools had not been introduced here at this time. Therefore, the role of the primary school and a measure of it success, might be seen as securing as many scholarships to grammar school for its pupils as possible.

John's relative autonomy at his schools is explained in that the 1944 Education Act also gave governors and head teachers control of the school curriculum and resourcing. It had said virtually nothing about the content of the curriculum other than Religious Education. John's championship of the traditional education was contrary to certain contemporary ideas and practices which were regarded as positive by some. In brief, these ideas and practices can loosely be defined as the move towards more informal, child-centred education with an emphasis on individualisation and learning by discovery: in short, a 'progressive' style of education.[9]

John and Eileen's marriage is described as one of equals and a true partnership. Yet Eileen's career took a completely different path to John's. She was obviously very intelligent and, as John proudly confirms, on leaving school, she passed the examination to achieve a very good position in the Civil Service. Yet, on her marriage the position had to be given up by law and like many women of her generation she did not work in paid employment until such time as her children were sufficiently grown up. This was the norm rather than the exception. For the wife and mother during wartime and the post-war period, work within the home was time consuming: the modern conveniences we take for granted were unheard of. The shortages of austerity meant that the skills of dressmaking, fruit bottling and overall the virtue of thrift were highly prized rather than the life-style choice they might be for some today. By the end of the 1950s sociologists Alva Myrdal and Viola Klein had identified the emergence of a 'dual role' for women. This model recognised the significance of women's domestic role and also confirmed the possibility of returning to serious participation in the workforce as the children grew older. The 1950s also saw the rise of the

---

[9] For some of the detail described here we acknowledge the assistance of Derek Gillard (2011) *Education in England: a brief history* www.educationengland.or.uk/history

'companionate marriage' where husbands and wives held equal status within marriage: a model exemplified by John and Eileen.[10]

The University of Winchester prides itself on its values, stating that 'Our values make us different'. In brief the University of Winchester values freedom, justice, truth, human rights and collective effort for the common good. We can't suggest that John learned these values from his time at King Alfred's College in the 1930s. His memoir emphasises that they have been with him all his life. That he has practised them with such distinction is what makes him a very special alumnus.

Andrea Jacobs

University of Winchester

---

[10] See Richard M Titmuss, *Essays on 'the Welfare State'* (London: Allen &Unwin,1958).

Introduction

This is more like an explanation than an introduction, but one that I feel that I should make.

I was asked to think back and record some memories of my life, for the family. This I did, in a very general sort of way, off the cuff, and keeping mainly to my own experiences. It was decided to print from the musings on the discs and my daughter Eileen found someone who undertook the task of sorting out the recordings into some sort of chronological whole. It cannot have been easy to make something of the rambling recordings. Had I intended a biography from the start I would have much more about my family, in which I take such pride, in particular about our son John and daughter Eileen and their families, and about friends.

Our children gave us no problems as they grew up. They proceeded to college and university and now in their own retirement, they give me support that is the envy of so many people. Eileen is extremely busy in many ways, and is retired after a successful career. With her husband John, she lives in an interesting house which contains fifty grandfather clocks in Birstwith, the village where Eileen and I lived for many years, and where our grandson Simon now lives in our old house with his family. John lives in Cambridge with Barbara, and as I write they are converting the house next door, which they own, into two flats; one for themselves. John has had, and still has, a busy life and at seventy-three he still glides, and still plays football, probably twice a week.[11] I have a large family, with grandchildren and great-grandchildren, and I receive kindness from them all.

As I recorded my memories I kept constantly thinking of Eileen my wife. She was of course the greatest influence on my life, and I was unable to record in detail the span of some twelve years leading up to her death eight years ago. I tried, but I was not successful. She was diagnosed with Alzheimer's disease around 1996, and we immediately set to work to offset it as much as possible. This entailed up to two hours, on most days, of sundry mental exercises and physical activities. She continued to do this for about nine years, struggling to offset the cruel disease, without ever complaining once. For years she travelled monthly to York to work with a Psychiatrist for an hour or so, and for many years very few people knew of her troubles. At this time, our daughter was a great help, and how can I forget the efforts of Georgina, our granddaughter, when she practically gave up her summer holiday to obtain, prepare and feed lunch to her Grandma every day. At some time in the future she may live in that house and bring up her family there. At present, Simon lives in it with his wife Julie, and their daughter Honey. I must mention, as an example of the support that I get, that they visit me in the care home where I live and have me back to supper on a weekly basis at the house where I

---

[11] Both John and his daughter Eileen advised us that at the Wales v England international football match for veterans in April, 2017, John (Senior) performed the ceremonial kick-off in which his son John (Junior), then aged 75, was playing.

spent so many happy years with Eileen. Eileen, who was a gold medallist in Elocution, lost her power of speech about six months after she had had to retire to bed, and for another two and a half years could neither speak nor eat solid food. She never once indicated, in any way, that she was in any difficulty and of course endeared herself to all who came to assist her, and I should pay tribute to all who helped me in caring for Eileen, and beg anyone who may read this to understand how much difficulty I had in dwelling on this time.

It is then a sketchy work, dealing very briefly with odd things that have made up my life. It is not intended to be rounded and complete, and there is so much more that I could say, particularly about some of the people who have been a part of my life and helped me throughout that life. To all of those people I say, "Thank you". It has been a simple but great journey, and as I have undertaken it, as I was taught by my parents and my school, I have always done a little simple voluntary work of one sort or another. It is my intention, if possible, to continue with this until I am a hundred later in the year.

Post Script to the original Introduction further acknowledging the role of Eileen and his children in his life:

I was repeatedly pressed to record for my family some of the anecdotes they had heard from time to time in conversation and to add to these others that might be of interest. Eventually I agreed to do this and over a considerable time I recorded a large number of stories in a fairly haphazard manner. This was really for my son and daughter and possibly other members of the family and therefore does not give my idea of what I owe to my remarkable family.

With this haphazard collection of recordings turned into memoirs, it is possible that the reader may not fully appreciate how much I owe to my wife, to my son and to my daughter. My wife, Eileen was remarkable in every way, never giving a thought to herself. She was respected and loved by everybody who knew her, most of all by me, who knew her when she was 16, until she died when she was 89. She has scarcely left my mind in the last eight years. My children, John and Eileen, have inherited most of their mother's qualities and to this day give me any assistance I may need. It is probably due to their mother's character that never at any time through so many years have there ever been harsh words between us. I am sure they would join me in my tribute to her. [12]

---

[12] e mail from John Shannon to Andrea Jacobs dd 23.8.17

Chapter One: Childhood

I am John William Shannon. During the First World War, a German Zeppelin airship was brought down over Billericay within sight of 26 Harper Road, Barking, Essex, where I was born on 1 October 1916. This was the house of my maternal grandparents, and from where we could hear Bow Bells if the wind was in the right direction, which means that I am a cockney. My mother and father also lived there as well as my mother's two sisters, Aunt Bill (Lily, who became my godmother) and Aunt Jane. At other times, my grandmother had lodgers in the house too. We lived there for some time, in a small part of the house, before we moved to another house in Barking to St. Audrey's Road.

My three brothers were all born after me. George went into the Navy and became an Admiral, and at the end of his career he served for a time at the Admiralty. He later returned to work as Manager of Britain's Space Laboratory. Dan the third one, became a senior HMI and later number three at the Ministry of Education serving in the Advanced Projects Division under Mrs Thatcher. He wanted to become a potter and was buying a pottery in the Cotswolds, but sadly he died aged fifty-six just after he had handed in his resignation. Mike, the youngest of us, joined the Marines, but he bought himself out when he found he couldn't get the promotion that he had hoped for, despite the fact that he was the youngest colour sergeant in the whole of the Marine Corps. He ended up as a merchant banker working mainly out of Nigeria for a long time until he retired from that at around the age of forty-seven; but he then also returned to work.

My father first met his future father-in-law, John Haley, when he was just a young lad, as he used to clean out his stables. My mother's father had a haulage business, mainly furniture removal, I believe; and he also had a coffee shop which my grandmother ran. During the First World War, my father served in Belgium with the forerunners of the Commandos in a unit led by Charles Rumney Samson, where their duties involved dashing behind the enemy lines to gather information. The unit was known as 'Samson's Cars'. My father eventually became a Warrant Officer in the Royal Marines, where as a young officer he had a Marine brought before him for not properly saluting him the day before, when the Marine pointed at him and said, 'I know you, you're Bill Shannon, you used to muck out my horses.' This was quite true, and when my father was next home on leave he went to see this man, and a little girl opened the gate to him, and that little girl eventually became my mother and the Marine and his wife became my grandparents. My grandfather was for those days a very big man. He was about six feet two inches tall, and strong and large. His wife was only about four feet seven inches tall but she kept him firmly under her thumb, and she was very definitely in charge of the household. My mother had won a prestigious scholarship to go to grammar school, but had had to stay at home to help her mother following the death of a brother.[13] She then took up music and studied to be a concert pianist, but she gave it all up when she married my father. My mother was later the first lady postwoman in Britain.

A few months after I was born we went to live in St. Audrey's Road, as I said, and then my mother and I followed my father up to Dalmeny near Edinburgh where he was posted to the battleship HMS *Lion*. This was just after the Battle of Jutland, and I actually learnt to speak in Dalmeny so that when I was a very small boy I had a Scots accent apparently. I don't know how long we stayed there exactly, but my mother had a row with her landlady and so when my father came ashore he found that we had left our lodgings and gone back to Barking. We moved a lot when I was little, following my father about, and I am told that I went to eight schools before I was ten. We moved back to St. Audrey's Road from Edinburgh, and then to Chatham, and I can vaguely remember the school in Chatham. From there we went to Deal and Worthing, and eventually back to Barking. We lived in Harper Road when I was four where I went to North Street School, and by the time I was five I was expected to walk to school by myself. The school was about

---

[13] The comparatively few grammar schools for girls at this time would be fee paying except for a handful of scholarships. As John explains later in this chapter grammar schools did not become free to attend until after the 1944 Education Act when attendance could be achieved by passing the 11+examination. As late as the 1930s, about ten per cent of elementary school pupils were being selected to go on to secondary schools. The rest either remained in 'all-age' schools or went on to senior schools. See also the foreword and Gillard D (2011) *Education in England: a brief history* www.educationengland.org.uk/history

half a mile away over two railway bridges, and of course I had to come home for lunch, because in those days all ordinary schools closed their gates and locked them for two hours in the middle of the day. Then I walked back to school after lunch, and came home again at about four o'clock. That's what school was like for little children in those days.

When father came out of the Marines he decided to set up in business for himself. His ambition was to start a taxi firm in London, and we moved to a mews with garages in Hampstead near Primrose Hill, where we lived over the garages. The only thing I know about this venture is that it was a complete failure, and I suppose he must have lost most of his money because he then became a taxi driver working mostly for other people. He always wanted to work and did all manner of things during his life. He tried to be a fruit farmer at one time and a mushroom farmer, then a chicken farmer, then a builder and with my Uncle Jack he got some experience in the building line, but none of his activities ever came to anything. I suppose that my father was first and foremost a Marine. He was called back into the Marines during the Second World War where he later became the Company Commander of 45 Commando in the holding battalion at Marine Headquarters, Lympstone, Hampshire. Then towards the end of the war, because of the shortage of trained men he trained as and became a bomb disposal officer working between Exeter and Plymouth. He served in the Boer War, the First World War and the Second World War and had medals from all three, and he has a display in the Royal Marine Museum at Southsea.

Whilst we were in Hampstead I went to a private infants' school, a small school run by a French lady. I was six and I remember it quite well, funnily enough. I can remember how at break time the French lady lifted up a trap-door in the floor and disappeared downward and you saw her go down, step by step, and her head went down in jerks. But because the taxi business was failing I was not able to remain at a private school for long, and I was sent to the local state school which had a high wall around it. This lasted until my father discovered that the school was next to a sewage farm, when he moved me to a school at Chalk Farm. Chalk Farm School is still there and it is still a school. We were coming back from a garden party at Buckingham Palace in 2014 (to which I had been invited for my voluntary work) and we passed it by chance. I mostly remember the school, because whilst I was there I used to play cricket for another school where my teacher sent her son. I turned out for them at the weekends as if I went to his school, which was cheating really.

You may be beginning to wonder how I ever learnt to read, what with moving between all these different schools, but after being at Chalk Farm School for a certain amount of time I took the Bluecoat Scholarship Exam. Bluecoat schools were started to educate working-class children, and there was one nearby.[14] I passed and got a London County Council scholarship, but I wasn't able to take it up because we then moved back to

---

[14] Bluecoat schools were charity schools, the first of which was founded in the 16th century. The pupils originally wore a distinctive blue uniform.

Barking where I returned to North Street School. I was back at the school where I had first started, now aged about nine and a half, and I was put in the class of a man called Mr Anderson. He was an extremely good teacher and, in his wisdom, he decided to put me in for the local Essex Scholarship Exam a year early. I was about ten when I took it and I did fairly well and won the Jackson prize for being top of all the entrants for the scholarship exam, in that part of Essex. This scholarship allowed me to go to Barking Abbey School, a grammar school, where I stayed until I left school. This was a fairly new school and it had a very good head teacher. Nobody could get into the school unless he had won a scholarship and so the standard of work done at the school was considerably higher than in most schools. It was a first-class school, it had a very good intake and it was very well run. [15]

Many people reading this memoir perhaps won't realise that at that time most grammar schools in the country were fee-paying, and remained fee-paying for very many years. There was very little secondary school education available for people who couldn't pay school fees, but the Abbey School was an unusual school. It was known as a Circular 13/14 School and was one of only two schools in the country taking part in an

[15] John has advised us that: 'This grammar school was extremely well run by Colonel Loftus, who was made a general during the war. Now, a hundred years later o, he has had some of his 'valuable' educational ideas quoted. When he left Barking Abbey School, he went to teach in Africa. He retains the world record for the longest serving teacher in Africa. I corresponded with him until he was over 90'.

experiment. One had to pass the scholarship exam to get into the school but then one's school fees were paid on a sliding scale according to parental income, so that a parent might pay nothing or anything up to ten guineas a term. It doesn't sound much, but the sum of ten guineas was a lot of money in those days, and pupils could only stay at the school if their parents paid the amount according to their income, which the Government had ordered them to pay. I suppose as a consequence I never knew for sure whether I could carry on at the Abbey School the following year, and looking back on it I realise that this was quite a worry because I liked school. But in truth, I don't actually remember anybody who left school on account of their fees not being paid.

I first went to the Abbey School when I was ten years old. I remember that on my first day my mother, wanting to send me in my best clothes, sent me in a pair of short velvet trousers with little white buttons up the side. Of course, I was the only boy there wearing such trousers, and to her eternal credit when I went home at lunchtime she allowed me to take them off and put on an ordinary pair. My parents bought a new house in Barking at this time. It was a house built under the Small Dwellings Acquisition Act and was a modern, three-bedroomed house with integral hot water boiler and a garden, all for £625.[16] It cost £625 because our house was at the end of the block, otherwise it would have cost £600. I joined the local

[16] Under the Small Dwellings Acquisition Act, local authorities lent money for the purpose of acquiring ownership of private property.

church choir with my brothers, where we had to perform at two services on Sundays and we also practised twice a week. We had piggy-back fighting contests behind the church, and I remember being the local piggy-back fighting champion! I don't remember who my 'horse' was but anyway, we won, and at that time that was what was important!

For my first three years at the Abbey School I came top of the 'A' stream, but I lacked maturity, being younger than everybody else in my year. I enjoyed school life but I would have done much better had I been just a little bit older. By the fourth year I had become quite blasé, I didn't find the work very difficult, and I had become mad on sports. When I came second in the 'A' stream I took my Report Book home that day. This was a journal we had to keep and which our parents had to read and sign weekly. I gave it to my father, showing him that I had come second, and he looked at it and said, 'Not much to your credit, is it?' I can remember now the effect that that small comment had on me. I was quite shattered, and I feel that from that moment on something changed. I could do enough work to get by and I passed the various exams, but it changed my attitude towards academic work. I realise that it shouldn't have done, but it did. At that moment, I think that any pretensions I had to real "work" left me.

The Abbey School maintained a good standard in everything and it is where I developed my love of sport. The school was very good at sports. All the boys had to do Boxing regularly and took part in Boxing competitions, and because we were a

Boxing school we produced many London and some National Boxing Champions. We also had the England Schoolboy Football captain, when the Headmaster issued a challenge, at one time, to any school in the country to come and play his Football team. He would have liked a good Cricket team, but we never really had one, although we did have the County Cricket Schoolboy Captain at the school. The school was co-educational in name only. There was an equal number of girls and boys but the girls studied at one end of the building and the boys studied at the other. We had our own separate entrances. The separation of the sexes was total, but physical education for both boys and girls was compulsory. All the girls had to do Judo, and we also had an incredibly good Girls' Hockey team, and whilst I was there two of the girls played for the Ladies' County Hockey team. So, standards were high and failure was not an option. This was in the days when people were actually failed in examinations. Despite being mad on sport I took nine GCSEs and two more later, and then took four higher school certificates (the equivalent of 'A' levels today).[17] When my son John was with me for a function at The Abbey School once, he looked up and saw my name up on the school Honours' Board in gold lettering, and said, 'Here Dad, is that you up there?' It was, but it wasn't much really.

---

[17] The equivalent of GCSEs in the 1930s would be the School Certificate which was established in 1918. GCEs were established in 1951 and replaced by GCSEs in 1988.

If my family could have afforded it I would have gone to University, but in those days, of course, you had to pay and so towards the end of my schooling it was decided that I should take the Civil Service Administration Examination, and aim for a senior post in the Civil Service. However, as luck would have it, the year I was going to sit the exam in 1934 it was cancelled. For the only time in its history it was cancelled, and I was left high and dry, and left with the problem of what to do next. We talked about it at home. I was too young to apply to go to college or university, for which you had to be eighteen in those days. I went for an interview for a job with a printing firm in London where I was told that I was far too educated for the job they needed doing. Then somebody said to me, 'Why don't you do student teaching for a year and then take the admin examination next year?' I thought that this would be a good idea. One got paid for being a student teacher (very little, but one did get paid), and to my surprise I liked teaching, and in fact liked it very much. My week consisted of four days' teaching experience helping out at a secondary school and one day back at my old school where I could do whatever I liked that I thought would help me. I chose to do mainly Woodwork and a little bit of Metalwork, as well as games of course. I was seconded to a good school with a splendid headmaster who put me with an absolutely first-class teacher, and I learnt a very great deal there. In the final term, I was allowed to take over the class, teaching the form work of the teacher who was helping me, and I thoroughly enjoyed it. So much so, that I decided that I would like to apply to go to college to become a teacher. This I did in 1935.

Chapter Two: Eileen

Eileen Winifred Galbraith was born in Barking at 85 Faircross Avenue on January 9, 1919, about two hundred yards as the crow flies from where I was born.[18] *Barking then a very respectable working-class town in Essex: every door knocker would be polished daily. Every doorstep would be whitened and many families would go to the bandstand in the park on Sunday afternoon. Eileen's grandmother, a widow who owned the house would always go, in her high lace up boots and large hats. The aunties would prepare the Sunday lunch. Grandfather might stroll down to The Creek to see his friends.* She was born whilst her father Alan was an officer with the Army of Occupation in Germany, and after her birth she went with her mother Winifred straight to Germany where they lived for about two years. She then moved with her family to India where she lived until she was seven and a half. *Her father had obtained a well- paid job, which was to lead to a very highly paid position*

I was told by Eileen that her mother cared for her inclusively and would not allow an Indian Ayah to look after her, or allow any Indian to touch her food. It was probably not to Eileen's

_____

advantage but her mother was completely protective of her. [19]
Her life was excessively sheltered and her mother sheltered her from all Indian influences completely.

Eileen, as a baby, with her parents

---

[19] John has advised us that Eileen's mother cared for her entirely and taught her to read, to write, to sing and to dance.

Eileen had her own rickshaw Boy, who took her three times a week to a little playgroup in the nearby town, but other than those few playmates she was screened from contact with virtually everybody. *There was one occasion when she had to go out and her mother by pure fortune found out that the Boy had been ill and his brother had done the ten-minute task. Eileen was immediately immersed in potassium permanganate and was brown for days.* It must have been a strange environment for a little girl to grow up in, and of course sadly, it meant that she had no friends as a young child.

Mrs Galbraith was a very considerable singer and she had a splendid voice. She used to sing at the cathedral in Calcutta, and she also sang on the radio in Calcutta during the Second World War, where she became a sort of sweetheart to the Forces in the East. Eileen was also a very competent singer for a child, and also danced, and danced with a group for the Toc H charity in various parts of India.[20]

I know this because I have a photograph of her at about five or six when she was dancing on her *pointes*, and I know that her mother was very keen on this. At the age of seven and a half however, Eileen was put on a passenger liner by herself for the five-and-a-half-week journey to Tilbury.

---

[20] Toc H is an international Christian movement originally established to provide rest and recreation facilities for soldiers in the First World War. It developed into an interdenominational association for Christian social service.

Eileen, as a girl, dancing

She was met by family members she didn't know and taken to live in Ilford. This did not work. Apparently, the elderly aunt found that her paying guest was too much responsibility, as the mother was concerned to watch over every detail of her life from thousands of miles away. There is no gainsaying her concern. Eileen had to move.

Back in Britain, her grandmother was incapable of caring for Eileen on her own, and so her Aunt Mabel ('Jo' to everybody) left work to help to care for her back at 85 Faircross Avenue. *Really this worked very well. True a young girl with an elderly widow and two spinsters did not seem ideal but it worked. Eileen must have been a very amenable child.*

Eileen did not go to school until her mother came home on leave the following year when she was sent to the Ursuline High School for Young Ladies. *Eileen was about eight and a half when she entered the High School. These years were absolutely packed with activity. At home, the general routine was governed by mum from India and she had nothing but her daughter's benefit at heart. School was busy indeed, and it took a tram ride and two walks to get there. Homework was compulsory and Eileen was very diligent. The school was a convent school and rules were very strict but suited Eileen on account of her upbringing. Dancing, needlework, music, acting were all a huge part of the curriculum and this pleased her too. Of course, she played games and swam and was a regular at the open-air gym in Barking where she built up the strength to wrestle any boy about her own size.*

She worked hard at school and caught up with her peers until at the age of fifteen she passed the equivalent of her 'O' level exams with distinction. She took up elocution lessons whilst at school, as well as acting and music, and very early in the fifth form she became the school pianist: *a coveted post in a school where almost all the girls played the piano.* She was also the leading lady in productions of the school's Dramatics Society.

Eileen looked forward to the sixth form. It was not to be, because her father had suffered a huge loss and lost his post through no fault of his own. There was no money for the sixth form to be completed but enough left from the ruin for one year at St George's, the crammer for the Higher Grades of the Civil Service. It was normally a three-year course. After about a year she left and waited to take the exam. It was a national competitive exam mainly fought out at the top by people who had spent two years at establishments like St George's.

Where did we meet? Well, we met at a Pancake Party at St. Paul's Church in Barking, when Eileen was sixteen and I was just about to go off to college in 1935. Her mother was singing at the party, as she was home on leave at the time without Mr Galbraith, and was just about to go back to India. Eileen's parents lived in India altogether for forty-three years, but her mother came home when Eileen was fifteen or sixteen I think, and stayed for the better part of a year. Eileen didn't see her mother or her father again until she was twenty-five or twenty-six, when she was herself a mother with two children.

Well, her mother was singing at this party and Eileen was with her, hidden away in the corner behind the piano. So, I danced with her mother and was cunning enough to ask Mrs Galbraith if she would introduce me to her daughter, which she did, and that is how we met. We met once or twice after that during my college vacations and became fairly friendly. It was a friendship that grew as and when I was about in the holidays and it was completely platonic. That is perhaps difficult to understand today, but for the next two and a half years we were simply very good friends, and we did a number of things together. We played tennis quite a lot and Eileen was a good tennis player. We went for walks and we went to amateur dramatic clubs. She went on with her acting. I didn't go to her club as I wasn't any good, but I went to a local one where I mainly swept the floor and things like that, but of course I went to her performances. Eileen carried on with her elocution and won a national contest, gaining a Gold Medal in Elocution from the Royal Academy. She belonged to a choir. I didn't go to the open-air gym but Eileen went there a great deal, so that she was exceptionally strong for her slim build. I played a lot of football and cricket.[21] We did work connected with our churches but we went to different churches, and sang in different choirs. We were friends. It's a difficult thing to describe, but we were just very good friends. We had similar likes and dislikes.

---

[21] Speaking elsewhere, John has admitted that,' When I was young, I was mad on football; I just lived from one game to the next'.

We had no money of course. Eileen wore clothes that her mother had made and sent over, and thinking about this with hindsight it must have been rather difficult for a young woman when she was eighteen or nineteen to be still wearing clothes that her mother had made for her. However, they were good clothes as her mother was a talented dressmaker, and they were made with the most beautiful Indian fabrics which meant that she looked elegant and was the envy of all her friends. Of course, she didn't like her clothes, but she had no money to buy any others. When we could do something together we did so, but in the mean time she was becoming the belle of our social circle, and when we met during vacations I thought that I was just someone on the fringes. We did everything together when I was at home, but we were just friends, and I thought that things would undoubtedly come to an end. But we carried on seeing each other.

Our son was once told by one of her contemporaries that as a girl Eileen was so pretty that it wasn't fair, nobody else had a chance. Eileen was first class academically, a singer, a dancer, an elocutionist, a distinguished actress, a local tennis champion and a first- class table-tennis player. She intended to go on to train to be a teacher but in 1929 the financial crash happened and her father's job disappeared, and what had been a fairly wealthy family suddenly became a very poor family. The opportunity for her to carry on at school and then to college to train to become a teacher was no longer open to her due to the family finances. Despite this the Galbraiths found enough money to send Eileen up to London to St. George's College for a two-year course, to undertake the competitive examination for the Civil Service that I had wanted to do. They negotiated that she would do the course in one year instead of two, and at the end of this crammer course she took the national examination and came twenty-ninth in the country. Ranked just a little higher and she would have gone directly into the Diplomatic Corps, but as it was she went into the Inland Revenue at a high grade. She was on very poor pay but she had a good career ahead of her. At the age of nineteen, in the days when women in such positions were very rare, by national competitive entry she had gained an employment where she had forty-six men junior to her. As an example of what she was doing she had under her jurisdiction the books of Henry Hughes & Sons, quite a large industrial company and one of the country's best makers of fine engineering instruments. Their executives must have been surprised.[22]

But of course, Eileen was unable to be a teacher, and that is what she had really wanted to do. At sixteen she had had a Sunday School class of twenty children and she carried this on for a while and did the job very well. This was at the time when her father's prospects were extremely good, and when they lived up to their position. I understand that at one time in the compound where they lived in India they had a large house and eleven servants to look after them, including the chauffeur

---

[22] John has advised us that: 'When I was due in Aberdeen, during the war and before we were married, the men under Eileen in her department had a 'whip round' and collected enough money for her to have a day off and come up to Aberdeen to see me. They were very proud of her'.

whose sole job was to take her father down to his office and bring him back in the evening. But all this wealth was gone and Eileen had to make her own way in the Civil Service.

Meanwhile her parents were struggling in India. I know very little about this time, but being poor whites in India under the Raj must have been very difficult. They had been very charitable people when they had had money. In later conversations, I discovered that they had probably given half their income away and done a great deal of good. They practically sustained a small leper colony on their own, and they helped their Church a great deal as well as giving to other charities in India. They were very good people but practically, they were unable to take care of themselves.

After she joined the Civil Service, Eileen dropped Elocution and a great deal of her music and dancing but she carried on with her acting and joined the Bercinguen Players, a London Amateur Repertory company. During the time she was with them, she was automatically the leading lady, whether it was being a young flapper of eighteen, an old lady of seventy who had killed her husband, or Elizabeth Barrett Browning in 'The Barretts of Wimpole Street'. She was an exceptionally good actress. Eileen also still sang with the Bernard Baron choir, who were a good London choir. Essentially, people's lives at that time were governed by apprehension and the threat of war. We qualified for First Aid, and Eileen qualified for Air Raid precautions duty which she did, in a big way, when the war broke out. Our lives were overshadowed by the fact that war was imminent. *Every home had to have an air raid shelter built.*

Eileen helped dig out theirs at 85, Faircross Avenue, where she still lived.

Chapter Three: College

When it was decided that I would go to college to do Teacher Training I applied to go to King Alfred's College in Winchester. At that time, there were quite a number of colleges that were well known as being good colleges of education, and King Alfred's was one of them. It was a small college, but it had a good reputation. In 1935 the entrance qualifications for a college were roughly the same as for a university, but the plain fact was that generally speaking people who couldn't afford to go to university didn't go. I managed to pay my college fees by borrowing money from the County and from a trust. [23] My parents provided me with some pocket money even though they had three more children and no money to spare, and I worked or did voluntary work in the vacations.

Many students already had an intermediate Bachelor of Arts qualification before they went to college. One could get one's intermediate BA then, by having four higher school certificates, which excused you from taking an intermediate BA or BSc exam. Good colleges like Winchester attracted people who had those qualifications before they went. What of the work done at the college? Well, the staff set the academic standards, of course, and the college was affiliated to Southampton University. Southampton degrees could be had by taking a

---

[23] Elsewhere, John has stated that he obtained a loan from the Thomas Wall Trust. The first letter he received after the end of World War II was from the County Education Committee telling him he owed them part of his loan. The Thomas Wall Trust had cancelled his outstanding debt with them.

three-year course but the ordinary teaching certificate took two years. The work was of the same standard as the degree course but it had a shorter syllabus. Few people could afford to stay on for another year, but some did. I would estimate that under ten percent stayed on and took their degree. Students taking the ordinary teaching certificate took one advanced subject which was done at the degree level, as well as English, Maths, History or Geography, and compulsory Physical Education. Then there were the professional subjects such as the Teaching Practice done with groups of children, and the Technical Exercises where one taught for a short while with the whole year looking on, after which there was a discussion about how one had done and how it could have been done better. The college had about a ten percent failure rate because the standard was so high. It was a full programme. I took two advanced subjects, and got a distinction in both of them, although only an oral distinction in French.

Most people travelled by train in those days, and when the students first arrived at Winchester station we then had to carry our luggage, usually a large suitcase or a small trunk, the mile and a half to college. This was mostly up hill and we carried our luggage on our shoulders. When I think back on this today I find it very difficult to believe, but only comparatively wealthy people could afford to hire a luggage handcart from the station.

The student accommodation was all on campus in large, old houses. The accommodation varied and some people had

John 2nd row, 3rd from right on the steps of St James' Hall

rooms and some were housed in a dormitory with wooden partitions between the beds, and all the Senior Year were housed in a hall of residence which was called The Court. My friends and I lived for the first year in St. James' Hall, where I shared a room with Don Skingley (who later became my best man) and a man called Joe Poyner who had been Captain of the Gloucestershire hockey team.

One of the first things we did was to have a photograph taken of the whole Hall, with twenty or so students sitting on the steps outside the hall, and each year afterwards at College Reunions we took the same photograph with those present sitting in the same places. Gaps gradually appeared over the years until at the end I was left entirely by myself sitting on a step!

We went down to the dining room in the main building for our meals. The food was plentiful but ordinary, and not particularly varied or particularly good. The staff took their meals in the same dining room, but on a dais separated from the students where they ate much nicer meals. I imagine that this wouldn't go down well with today's students, but we accepted it: that was just what college was like. Everybody had his own place to sit in the dining room, which he had to keep. We had to sit in the same place for every meal and we had to be there before the bell rang. We could never be late for a meal or there was an enquiry. Everything was very, very strict. There was a dining hall monitor, a student, who dealt with any problems that arose through people being late. One glance around the room and he could see if a student was missing, and who it was.

We very quickly learned that the day-to-day running of the college was in effect managed by the students, and that the staff weren't that much involved. There were roll-calls morning and evening, taken by one of the students and organised by one of the students. Deportment and conduct was organised by the students. Looking back on it, I think that the students probably felt that they were rather superior to the average of society, and that they had to conduct their lives in that way. No student was allowed to enter a public house within six miles of Winchester, and certainly not any night clubs. No student ever went for a meal out. I cannot recall any incidence of any student having a single meal out during the whole time I was there. I was there for two years and I certainly never had a meal out. We might have a cup of tea but that would be it. I remember once about a dozen of us went down to Sally Lunn's café and Don Skingley, who was always playing the joker, said to the waitress, 'Can I have a glass of water and a caraway seed please?' Well, the rest of us were given our tuppenny cups of tea, but he didn't get anything and after a while he said to her, 'Have you got my glass of water and caraway seed?' And she said, 'I'm sorry, sir, but we're out of caraway seeds today.' That little cameo sticks in my mind for some reason. Very few students at the college had any money. None of us even owned a bicycle.

A student committee, headed by somebody called 'The Bishop', was very anxious that our college should be seen by everybody everywhere to be upholding good standards. Even on a Saturday we had to be back in college at a time which meant that we never saw the end of a film if we went out to the cinema. Our time at college was so busy and well organised, and so all-consuming, that it left no time for girlfriends, but in fact fraternising with the opposite sex was not allowed. If a student was seen consorting with a girl, then somebody would be bound to report it to the Bishop. The Bishop would hand out an admonition or punishment, and to be hauled up before the Bishop's Court was quite a bother, but his word or the Court's word was law. They set the standard in all matters. They cared for the standing of the college. They cared that students were there at roll-calls and made the bells. The staff ran the academic work, but college life as I have said before was run by the students themselves, and they wished to present a high standard to the public.

We didn't have an actual college uniform although at that time some colleges did, and most girls' colleges seemed to have one. But we did dress uniformly, because every single student wore a sober-coloured sports jacket, grey flannels and the college tie. We all wore the college tie: that was compulsory, or was made compulsory by the students themselves. You could therefore tell a student in town at a glance, and when students passed one another in town they would say, 'Cheerio.' It was rather like service personnel saluting each other. 'Cheerio.'

We weren't allowed radios in our rooms, or the means to make a cup of tea or coffee, and after six o'clock in the evening we couldn't get a cup of tea or something to eat from the dining room either. Looking back on it, all of this sounds impossibly severe but at the time we accepted it as being the norm and we got on with it pretty happily. It was perhaps a bleak life in many ways. The routine we had to follow was extremely strict and people today sometimes find it very difficult to believe it, when I describe to them how we lived and what was expected of us. Does it seem too restrictive, and did the students rebel? No, strangely perhaps these rules were accepted universally. We didn't mind, that was the strange thing about it.

Work went on again in the evening after a roll call. This could be lectures or private study, and continued until 'lights out' at ten-thirty pm. Yet we didn't mind that it was lights out at ten-thirty, when everybody had to be in his room. There were colleges at that time where even the staff had to be in and the doors locked by a certain time, which would be unbelievable today. But as a matter of a fact we were mostly pretty tired by ten-thirty as both physically and mentally we had had a hard day. Certainly, the work demanded of us was of a greater range than that demanded of students these days.

It sounds like a hard life but in actual fact everybody accepted it and I think that on the whole it was successful. We accepted that King Alfred's had high standards and was good at what it did, and that what we were doing was worthwhile. In those pre-war days King Alfred's thought that it was superior.

Perhaps it was. One thing that certainly comes from a lot of people being in one place and working to a common goal however is comradeship. There was a complete sense of comradeship. I cannot actually remember any bad feeling between the students. We were all in it together, we had chosen to be there, life was good and we believed in what we were doing. If something is done with good humour and good will, it works.

Sundays were different, although there were still roll-calls to check that everybody was in college, and there was lights out in the same way. No work was demanded on a Sunday but two religious services were held and everybody had to attend chapel twice. The rest of our Sundays were free, in other words, the afternoons were free but no sports were allowed on a Sunday. We had a splendid choir and a splendid organist. There was a college organ exhibition and quite a competition to take part, and I understand that over the years they had some top-class organists. Everybody had his own seat in chapel, just as in the dining hall, so that any absentee could be spotted immediately. It was compulsory to go to chapel, as I said, and it was also compulsory for everybody to take a turn at reading the lessons, which had to be read through to the Vice Principal on Friday evenings. I remember once running very hard to get to the Vice Principal's study in time to read a lesson when it was my turn. I went in and read the piece and not looking up from his page (he was a scholar and rarely left his room) he said, 'Well read, wrong lesson. Fined one shilling. Come back in an hour.' So off I went to find the right lesson, and then I had to go back and read it to him of course. The chapel was put out of use when the college expanded after the war and they built a new chapel. The new chapel was then given over to some other purpose, and the old chapel has just very recently been put back into use as a place of worship for the University of Winchester. The walls hold our academic honours, as well as memorials to former students killed in both world wars. In the First World War, the college had had an Officer Training Corps that formed a Company, with one of the lecturers as the Company Commander, and they were all lost in one of those terrifying battles of 1914-1918. I believe the whole Company was lost.[24]

Sport formed a large part of college life and was very enjoyable. The Principal interviewed all the applicants himself, and in fact I think it was his chief job as he didn't seem to do much else at the college when I was there. But he was very keen on Sport and prospective students were chiefly filtered by their sports ability. Lectures started with a roll-call in the morning and went on until lunchtime but in the afternoons, we were free to pursue our own activities which normally meant sport of one

---

[24] When war was declared in 1914, 104 students of the College Company (then known as B Company, 4th Hampshire Battalion, Territorial Army), were at annual camp at Bulford on Salisbury Plain. They were immediately mobilised and returned to the College until they were posted to India in December 1914. Thereafter the Company identity was gradually lost, but many members were involved in the campaigns in Mesopotamia and Palestine. 60 members of the College lost their lives during the war. See Tom James and Martin Doughty, *King Alfred's College Winchester: A Pictorial Record* (Stroud: Alan Sutton Publishing, 1991) 101.

form or another. In practice, this meant that even though we were a small college we could turn out teams in Rugby, Football, Tennis, Hockey, Badminton and Cross-country.[25] You name it we had it, and mostly they were quite good teams. We were young men of around nineteen to twenty-one years of age with energy and time on our hands which we spent training and playing, and we played quite a good fixture list. We typically had two Football match fixtures a week. We often travelled away for matches as far afield as Reading, Bristol, London, Portsmouth, Southampton and Birmingham. If we were at an away match we were allowed an extension of the evening roll-call, but this was only an extension and we weren't allowed out late. We had to get back by a reasonable time and check in. When we played away matches we went by bus and coming back we used to sing, but again the college name had to be upheld. We never sang when going through a village or a small town, it just wasn't done.

The sports field was at Bar End about a mile and a half away from college, and training was done on 'the Dytche', which has been completely built over today. We walked down to the

---

[25] The area of the University where John previously played tennis has been refurbished to be used as a multi-use games area (or MUGA – not the prettiest acronym) so other sports such as netball, hockey and football, as well as tennis, can be played on them. At the Winton Club Reunion lunch, on 24th June 2017, this area was officially opened by John, with the unveiling of a plaque as The John Shannon Sports Ground. The following day the inaugural John Shannon Tennis Tournament was played on the ground. The winners' names will be engraved on a shield he commissioned and donated to the University.

sports field of course, and walked back after the matches. I played football for the First XI until a minor knee injury caused me to stop and then Joe and Don, who were both county hockey players, took me under their wing and trained me until I got into the Hockey First XI where I didn't have to kick. So, in the second year I played hockey and enjoyed it.

John, bottom left, with hockey team

John, back right, with tennis team

I was also captain of both tennis and badminton, although I handed the badminton captaincy over to Len Williams, a great friend who later married Jean, a principal of Portsmouth College; and I was in touch with Jean until she died. I was also captain of chess, although it was a sort of nominal captaincy as I cannot remember ever playing a chess match. We possibly played a few matches against St. Mary's, the local school, where the old Wykehamists, as they were called, would have no doubt devoured us.[26]

I was the Treasurer of the Sports' Association, which probably took up five or six hours a week, although I had an assistant who actually did most of the work. As treasurer, I had to work with a member of staff called Tommy Atkinson and he was always trying to get permission to sign the cheques, and I had a jolly year battling him and refusing to let him sign them. He was a good bloke really, and I don't know what happened after I left but there is a University building named after him now. All the different sports had to pay for themselves, and there could be no question of debt. Everybody had to pay his share and the books had to balance out at the end of the year. Students paid for the sports they participated in, their kit and all of their own transport costs. In fact, looking back on it, I think that practically the only money the vast majority of students had at that time was spent on sport in one way or another, which would be inexplicable for young people today. But it was another world, wasn't it?

We had the privilege of playing tennis on three beautiful grass courts, over which I had control.

They were actually on the campus and were very fine courts surrounded by close, tall hedges, not by netting, and it was a privilege to use them. Of course, because of this I got to know

---

[26] The public school, Winchester College's Latin name is Collegium Sanctae Mariae prope Wintoniam (St Mary's College near Winchester).

the Head Gardener very well. Eileen and I later met him during the war. The college grounds themselves, I remember, were beautiful and covered in flowers, shrubs and trees. Some lawns were for the use of staff only and I didn't really like that, and don't think that it would be allowed today. They were quite exceptional grounds for those days. Now of course, they have been built over and form part of the campus of the new University of Winchester, where Alan Titchmarsh has recently been made Chancellor. He will no doubt be able to help plan the new campus grounds as it expands.

As regards other leisure pursuits, there was a Debating Society, and I remember belonging to the Irving Club which was a play-reading club, and about as near as I could get to the Dramatics Society. I wasn't ever very good at drama but some of my friends put on some excellent productions in the purpose-built theatre that we had at the college. There was an orchestra that always put on end-of-term concerts, and there were also on-the-spot concerts where talent of various sorts was put on show. I sang in a close harmony quartet once and that was great fun although we weren't very good at it. A couple of my friends were quite good musicians and they arranged the songs for us and we went on and sang them. We could play table-tennis and billiards in the Common room. We played all sorts of games there, but the facilities were rather poor. In fact, the Common room facilities altogether were rather poor, and I seem to remember that Common room games mostly involved young men letting off steam.

It being the 1930s, there were also Eugenics meetings run by the Principal, but these meetings rather stuck out like a sore thumb at our college. There were also lectures by outside speakers who came in to talk on quite a number of things throughout the year.

Another job I had at college was as curator of the post. You see, everything was done by the students. The curator of the post had a key to the college office which was a rather sought-after affair, not that it meant anything, but I could go to the college office and open up whenever I liked, and I was entrusted with a lot of little things. I had to see that the post left college each day, and that the post coming into college got sent out to the various Halls of Residence. It didn't take much time, and each evening except Sunday I used to walk down to the post box with my friend Ron Thompson. Ron was later a prisoner of the Japanese, and he then became a secretary of the Japanese Prisoners of War Association and worked for them all his life. In the last few years of his life he went backwards and forwards to Japan trying to build bridges between people. He said, 'We can't hate forever', and he was instrumental in fostering a reasonable *entente* between the Japanese, and the British soldiers still left who were their prisoners.

There were a number of characters among the staff, and the member of staff connected with the college office was the most mild-mannered and pleasant man I think I have ever come across. Later in my career I was involved with the National

Union of Teachers, and for many years wherever the NUT conference was held in the country, be it Blackpool or Bournemouth, Herbert Jarman would be standing at the door of the conference hall to spot 'his' men and shake them by the hand as they went in. He had an encyclopaedic memory for people and faces and knew everybody by name, which was not very difficult perhaps as the college wasn't a big place but apparently, he rarely missed an old Wintonian going into the hall. It was a task he had given himself. He was a very nice man and there is also a building named after him at the University of Winchester, as there is after Tommy Atkinson.

I think that generally King Alfred's turned out teachers who had been brought up to believe that teaching the young of the country was a worthwhile occupation. We had a good work ethic, a pre-disposition to do voluntary work, and to participate in sports, and most people thought that they had spent their time well there. We thought that to be a teacher was a good way of spending one's life, and on the whole, we were proud of the fact that our college trained teachers to do their jobs well, and most did it well. Some did it very well, certainly there were very, very many very successful teaching careers that sprang from the college.

We had a very full programme and most students did well, but of course in those days if one didn't measure up, one left. When I was there about eight or ten percent failed to complete the course, or left with a failure; some returned to do another year, or to take their exams another year. Two of my five close

42

friends failed and had to re-sit later. One of those who failed was a particular friend of mine who measured six feet six and three-quarter inches in his socks, which in those days was a positive giant of a man. He couldn't go on to teach because he had failed the course, and so he went up to the West End of London to be a gigolo in a private, very up-market club for very tall, wealthy girls, and he ended up marrying one of them. Another great friend failed and went off to teach without a certificate in a private school, and what I remember most about it was that he also had to clean the boys' boots. Unfortunately, I think that he became a very miserable man later on. My other room-mate, Don Skingley, went into the Army and served through the war and then stayed in the Army, but later moved to New Zealand.

We didn't all go in for teaching, of course. In my year there were about a dozen out of our group who did not do so. I could name an actor, a judge, the President of the Licensed Victuallers' Association, an author, someone who went into the Church, and a genealogist, whose daughter my son and I take each year to the College Reunion. Out of two students who went into the Army that I know about, one became a Colonel of a tank regiment and later became the Managing Director of the CBI or something like that and he had a large house in Bath, in the Circus.[27] He kept his rank from war time, Colonel Cunningham, which I thought was a bit of a cheek really, and it was only towards the end of his life that I discovered that he

---

[27] The houses comprising the Circus, Bath are Grade 1 listed.

had been in the Army all the while. These were all from fifty something college leavers. One student from my year who didn't become a teacher and who used to come to the college reunions at Winchester said to me, 'I couldn't meet what was expected of me as a teacher from King Alfred's'. This surprised me, but he obviously meant it.

I was there in 1935-1937, and if one visits the splendid University of Winchester today it is interesting to see the vestiges of the college that remain. There were about one hundred and fifty students when I was at college, and today the University has eight thousand students, and has just been awarded the funds to be able to *double* in size. Two of its main buildings are named after our college lecturers, the college pond was dug and built by my year, our college Exhibitionists' names are carved in oak in the Chapel, the Administration Block was first used by my college colleagues as accommodation, and we first used the Bar End Sports' Facilities, etcetera.

I have an anecdote from college which I think illustrates the ethos of the good pre-war Colleges of Education in the 1930s. We were at an English lecture being given by a young lecturer whose background was Cambridge and the BBC. He had been there about two years and was no doubt extremely well qualified, but he had very little idea about what we needed. I was sat just behind Trevor Woolf in the lecture hall, who was my right-hand man in the dining room where I was the head of a table. His job there was to cut up the butter into equal pieces and pass it around the table in such a way that he was the last person to have his share, which established that there were equal shares for everybody. About ten minutes into the lecture Trevor stood up and put his arm up, and the English lecturer stopped, and Trevor said, 'Sir, is it absolutely necessary for me to pass English for me to get my certificate?' 'Yes,' said the lecturer. Trevor looked at him slowly and then said, 'Then I'll go elsewhere and get some work done.' With this he slowly swept up his papers, picked up his books and walked slowly down the aisle and out through the door. Trevor was a committed Communist but he never said a word about it in public. He didn't allow his politics to intrude upon his college life, and was very professional. Politics were for one's private life: there were no banners ever put up and no political meetings held at the college. Trevor was an average student and not the best at games. He played of course, because one had to, but he also fished. He was the only student in the college that I remember who used to go off to the River Itchen fishing. That was his interest. So, it was an unusual incident, but it depicts how students on the whole were very concerned about doing well and getting a good teaching certificate. Nothing was said to Trevor, but the lecturer left at the end of the year, which was a good thing as he was actually pretty useless.

The college actively encouraged voluntary work, and we had Rag Days where we dressed up and collected money for charity, and volunteering days when we did things like visit prisons. I led a team that went prison visiting on Saturday evening to Winchester Prison, and a team also visited casual wards with

Toc H. 'Muffs and Duffs' was the day when sports were played for charity by students who didn't normally play them. So, the Tennis team would play the Cricket team at Cricket, the Soccer players played the Rugby players at Rugby, the Rugby players played the Hockey players at Hockey and so on. One afternoon in the summer was given over to that and it was great fun, and for a good cause.

Celebration of St Luke's Night

Then there was St. Luke's Night, when the entire college got into costume and paraded around town collecting money, again for charity. I recall being dressed up as a jockey, and riding a man dressed as my horse whose name was actually Steed.

Strangely not long ago his son got in touch with me and asked me if I could give him some information about his father. His father's house had been completely destroyed during the war and everything had been burnt, and he had no knowledge whatsoever of his father's time at college. Fortunately, I was able to give him a photograph or two and to give him quite a bit of information about his father. His father was religious, and very knowledgeable about religious history, and he took a seminar of five of our friends in order for us to try and pass the Archbishop's examination in Religious Studies. Everybody in the college was rather expected to take this exam, because for everybody who passed, the college got a grant from the Church, and so it was very popular. In fact, I don't actually remember the details, but I believe that it was almost compulsory. Anyway, Steed took the seminar and us yobbos listened to him and worked at it and we all passed. Five of us got 'A's or 'B's.

I ought to say a word more about the vacations both from school and college. As these were long I did various jobs in the holidays, both paid and voluntary, but mainly to try and take the financial burden off my parents. One summer holiday, when I was sixteen and still at school I painted the next-door neighbour's house back and front, and when I'd finished the neighbour gave me a sum of money. I can still remember my father being angry about it, because this sum worked out at something like sixpence an hour. I was the oldest of four, and I realised the sacrifices they were having to make to put me through college, so if I could get a few weeks of uncertificated teaching supply teaching that was all to the good. Because our vacations were longer than those of the state schools, in those days you could get uncertificated supply teaching, for which one was paid of course. One year I also did a bit of coaching at Martells Manor in Essex, where I coached a girl for her School Certificate. Then for the two years that I was at college I volunteered for a few weeks in the summer at the Plymouth Brethren camp for under-privileged children, that they set up at an RAF Lee-on-Solent camp near Southampton. The Plymouth Brethren would set up this big camp under canvas, that held about four hundred children from London as well as a whole army of helpers, very largely students. We spent quite a happy time there, and my job involved mainly playing and organising games with the children. There was no pay, but we were given our bed and board and it cost us nothing to go there.

Of course, colleges like King Alfred's disappeared with the war. Actually, in 1939 they disappeared never to return in the same set-up. Most of them grew of course, and their campuses expanded, and a number turned into universities. King Alfred's College of Education expanded and grew, and from it grew the splendid present-day University.

Chapter Four: Pre-War

After I left college in 1937 I went back home and applied to the Barking Education Committee for a job. Both Mr Anderson, who had been my teacher when I was nine or ten at North Street School, and Mr Nield who had been my headmaster when I was a student teacher at Eastbury School, said that they would like to have me on their staff. I only learnt about this some years later and apparently there was a bit of an argument about it, and like Solomon, the Director of Education (a man named Compton who also wrote quite good books on education) said, 'Well, Mr Shannon shall go to neither', and he sent me to Cambell School which was a secondary school in Becontree.

Cambell School was a large, new, boy's secondary school underMr Galley, and I was to be supernumerary for a year. This meant that he could use me anywhere in the school. As I was a PE and games fanatic I was to understudy the Head of the Physical Education Department, a man called Newton who ran a very good department. It was a wonderful opportunity and it suited me down to the ground. We had a big, new gym with all the equipment you could want, and the boys were as equally mad on playing games as I was. We put out life and soul into things, it was great. I was still playing a lot of football myself then, as well as a great deal of tennis and some cricket. I worked incredibly hard that first year.

John with Cambell School Football Team

Mr Newton was an exceptionally able man and I set out to copy him, and I determined that if I could, I would do things even better than he had. I was a bit self-opinionated, and looked for ways in which I could improve the department. Mr Newton was planning to leave as he had been head-hunted for a Civil Service post to head the organisation of Physical Education in His Majesty's Prisons, and for the last term of that first year he handed over his work to me to do and he 'floated'. It was my first year out of college but he allowed me my head, and when he left at the end of the year I had worked like a slave and possibly had actually improved the department a little. It was a splendid department, and to everybody's surprise at the end of

50

the year Mr Galley appointed me as its Head. I was quite worried about what the other members of the department would think, but they were apparently quite happy about it, all except one member of staff, who was the only man in the whole of my education career whom I ever really fell out with. I asked one of the other staff what I should do (this man was nearly twice my age), and he looked at me and thought and then he said, 'Hit him in the belly.' I didn't think that that was quite the way to go about it, but we managed to resolve things reasonably well in the end. In those days, departments didn't have paid heads, the Headmaster of the school just appointed people who he thought would be good to be put in charge of specific work in the school. The only teacher who got any extra pay was the Deputy Head. In addition to becoming Head of Department I got elected to be a member of the Southern Counties Physical Education Association on the strength of the work that we were doing there. You could only be invited to join by people who were well known people in the physical education field, people like Mr Newton!

In 1937, in addition to my new job I decided to qualify as a Play Leader. Play-leading was a scheme that was dreamt up at the end of the 1930s and was killed by the war, and has never been revived to the same extent. In fact, I doubt if many people know what it was. It was the dream of the National Council of Physical and Recreational Training. The idea was that town parks would be used to the advantage of children in the school holidays, so that instead of kicking around the streets children could undertake games such as Cricket, Netball, Rounders,

Basketball, Football, and other activities under a qualified Play Leader with helpers from the local district. A Play Leader was appointed to an area and then he had to find volunteers to help with the play scheme. He borrowed all the necessary equipment from local schools, who weren't of course using it in the holidays. The Local Education Authority gave instructions that the schools were to lend their equipment, and I believe that there was some agreement whereby if anything was lost or damaged it would be replaced to the school. But it was a very cheap scheme for the Local Authorities to run as all they really had to do was to pay a Play Leader, and after that he or she gathered in a whole range of voluntary help. The equipment didn't cost anything and the park didn't cost anything to hire, so it was a very cheap way of getting literally hundreds of children off the streets.

I had to go up to London in the evenings to train for this after work. The training was done at Tenison's Grammar School near the Oval, and it being those days this was done entirely at my own expense. I hoped that the course would help me in my career. I've forgotten for how long the course lasted but it was quite some time, and whilst I was doing it I met Sir Walter Winterbottom, later the manager of the England football team. In 1938, the first year I ran a Play Leading scheme, I went to Cirencester in Gloucestershire. My daughter Eileen still has a notice of the sort that they stuck on the lamp-posts saying that 'Mr Shannon, an expert of the National Council of Physical and Recreational Training, will be in the town for five weeks', etc. It is rather fun to look at now, and it did work well. I got help from students from the local Colleges of Education, I went around all the pubs and the skittle alleys and got help from there, and I got the local boxing club and local cycling club to help, and some parents volunteered. The Play Leading scheme was run on the City Bank Playing Fields and we didn't have any problems or bothers of any kind. I had many voluntary helpers, and the park held hundreds of young children, quite happily. Eileen came down to help me during her summer holiday.

The following year in 1939 the scheme was expanded and many parks up and down the country got involved. I ran the scheme for Edmonton in North London, where Eileen helped me again, and we got help from all over the borough. One day at the end of August, Eileen was alone in charge at Pymmes Park when a lot of soldiers arrived at the park and said, 'You'll have to move off here lady, we're going to put a barrage balloon up.' So, she had to round up all the children in a hurry. They didn't lose one ball, bat or stick. It was intended to extend the dream into Ilford the following year and as far as I know, seven parks were going to be used in Ilford. The whole play-leading scheme was rapidly expanding across the country and but for the war coming along, most moderately sized towns would have taken this up, and you would have had parks all over the country full of active children happily playing games and undertaking sports in their school holidays. The dream died with the war and was sadly never re-kindled, which is a great pity. I really don't know why no-one has really tried to get it under way again. It would be more difficult today, of course.

What else did I do as a young man? Well, I read voraciously and very widely. I took part in church activities. I still played football. I was never as good at football as I thought I was, as I wasn't big or strong enough. I did have one game with a big, amateur club, but afterwards they didn't even write and tell me that they didn't want me, and I thought that I'd done quite well. West Ham had two or three teams playing in the local leagues, and they put people in a team whom they were interested in, but I was quite obviously one of those who just made up the numbers and was never going to get any further. I suppose at times I might have thought that I could, but not very seriously. I went to evening classes quite a lot, and did some evening class teaching too. I ran a youth club in Becontree one night a week, that turned into quite a well-known boxing club after I was there. It was really a general youth club when I ran it. I used to visit the YMCA at Plaistow one evening a week with a group of friends. *The Red Triangle Club* it was called, and I believe it's still there. It had about five floors plus a basement and one could play badminton, swim, use the gymnasium or play table-tennis or billiards. You could do almost anything; and a party of us used to attend. We went there by train, which only took about a quarter of an hour. We did our own thing and then met up at the end for a cup of coffee before going home. It was a simple and very good way for a group of young people to spend the evening. I also went occasionally to the Bernard Baron settlement in Tower Hamlets as a visiting PE instructor, as a favour for a friend who did the Play Leading course with me. The Bernard Baron settlement was a Jewish settlement set up by a man called Bernard Baron, and our type of physical education was different from that which they normally had and they liked having a visiting instructor, and I met some very nice people there.

Every evening was taken up with something and the weekends were very full too. Many of the activities at that time of course I did with Eileen. We played a great deal of tennis and won the local doubles championship one year. Other activities I did with different friends, and a few friends remained friends for life. They have all gone now but they were friends with whom one felt easy and at home, and we were happy in each other's company. Life was completely full. As you will be aware, of course, there were no television sets then and no computers, no mobile phones, no iPads, no laptops and there were no clubs and pubs like young people go to today. Young people weren't allowed in pubs, and they never had a lot of money to spend anyway. They didn't go to bars and they didn't hang around restaurants and cafés. They certainly didn't go to nightclubs. Going clubbing had never been dreamt of, not for young people; not in our type of society anyway. There were nightclubs, but nightclubs were expensive and completely out of the reach of people like us.

This period of our lives, 1937-1939, became gradually dominated by the war. At the youth club I ran, one night those present were all talking about war. War was coming, everybody knew a war was coming, everybody could see it, and they decided to go down together as a body to the local Drill

Hall to join the Territorials. They asked me if I would like to go with them but I wanted to join the Navy, not the Army, and so I went off to London where HMS *President* was moored on the Embankment, and joined the Royal Naval Volunteer Reserve instead. When I joined up I actually wanted to be a signalman. It didn't work out that way, but that's what I had intended. In 1939, I was a member of the RNVR for a couple of months before the war broke out, and then when I reported back to HMS *President* I expected to be told to come back and get my uniform. However, I was told that the Government had decided that teachers from my area were to be given a month's grace to help with the evacuation of schoolchildren, so I had to go back to Barking and help to evacuate the children from Cambell School. Children who lived around London were all being evacuated.

That was an experience which I will never forget. The war was just about to start when they started the evacuation. Meetings were held in schools and arrangements were made, and all the children were given labels to tie onto themselves. I loved the meeting at our school where there were a lot of anxious parents in the hall, and one father asked the Head Teacher something about would they get much notice and would the children all be together. The head looked at him and said, 'Well, sir, how many children have you got?' And the man, who was standing up, looked down at his wife and said, 'How many is it Mary?' And Mary said it was six! Off we went, up to London with the crocodiles of children, where there were thousands of them carrying their gas masks in their little cardboard boxes, with their name tags hanging off their lapels describing who they were and where they came from. You did not know when you left where you were going. Children just boarded the next empty train that came into the station until it was full and the train then set off. Our lot got on a train, or two trains, and we were sent to Somerset. We were tipped out at Templecombe, where mostly ladies and a few men came to pick up the children who had been allocated to them. They came from all the villages round about, spread over quite an area. The children were dispersed and went to the nearest village school. The teaching staff were also allocated to hosts. I lodged with the Reverend Scott, who was the Rector of a tiny village called North Cheriton. A road ran up to the village and then stopped there. There was a church and not much more than a dozen houses I suppose, and one big house, and the rectory. Living there was just like being in a Jane Austen novel. The Rector's wife would ring the bell to fetch the maid into the room in order to pass a peach to the Master. The maid would come in and Mrs Scott would say, 'Pass the master a peach, Daisy.' The Master would be sitting in his chair, probably about three feet away from where the dish of peaches was placed whilst his daughters and his wife sat in straight, high-backed chairs doing their needlework. The maid, having given the Rector his peach on a plate, would then curtsey and disappear. Reverend Scott turned out to be an ex-naval Padre, and he later married Eileen and I in his tiny little church at North Cheriton one Sunday morning on January 26 in 1941. He was actually a thoroughly good chap and his family did a lot of good work in the district. I was at the rectory a month, during which time my job was to travel to all the villages round about, to Wincanton, Horsington, Templecombe, Henstridge, Bruton and all that area, seeing that the children were settled into a local school and had settled with their host families, interviewing the host parents and making changes where necessary and generally trying to be useful. After the month was up of course I reported back to the HMS *President* and was sent to Chatham. My war was about to start, and society as I knew it as a young man would never be the same again. Six years later things would be completely different.

Chapter Five: The Navy

Chatham barracks were completely overcrowded when I got there. I remember being told that there were twenty-four thousand sailors there at the time. It was difficult for the authorities to find anything for us all to do, and keeping everyone busy was a problem. Luckily, I was sent off almost immediately to Skegness, where with a party of a hundred or so others, I was to help turn Butlin's holiday camp into a naval training establishment. A pretty poor place it was too. The camp's summer chalets were only thin wooden huts with no heating, and we were on the East coast in winter. All we had was the usual naval issue of two blankets so we slept in our clothes, and there were no real washing arrangements. We had to take out all the old pedaloes, bicycles and other holiday camp equipment and ask the local farmers if they would allow us to store it in their barns. We moored rowing boats in the swimming pool for men to learn to row. We piled stuff up, took stuff out, cleaned up, cleared out, filled sandbags and built machine gun emplacements. It was a pretty grim job and nobody liked it, but we got the place ready to be used, and at the end of six weeks we went back to Chatham. We were hardly prepared for war!

Next, I was given the job of sweeping up leaves. Armed with a broom I was told to sweep up leaves on an enormous parade ground that was about half a mile long. We swept them into piles and then the wind blew them away, and then we had to sweep them up again, and we did that all day long. It struck me as being a futile exercise, and in fact I became very indignant about it and I applied for indefinite leave on the grounds that I was wasting my time, thereby creating history to some extent. I spoke to the Officer of the Watch and he said, 'Certainly not.' I said, 'Right, I'll go and see the Officer of the Day.' That is one of the good things about the Navy. Everybody has the right to be heard, and if a request is turned down he has the right to go to the next senior person and so on, right to the top. No-one thinks badly of a rating for doing it. So, then I saw the Officer of the Day and he said, 'Certainly not.' 'Right, I'll ask to see the Commander,' I said, and after I'd gone through the Commander and the Base Captain I reached an Admiral, and finally I found myself in a room before the Admiral with all his officers lined up in a row beside him. I was asked why I was there and I told him, and the Admiral said, 'Is this true?' And the Captain asked the Commander, and the Commander asked the Officer of the Day, and the Officer of the Day asked the Officer of the Watch, and the Officer of the Watch asked the Regulating Petty Officer, 'Is this strictly true?' And when the answer came back 'Yes', the Admiral roared out laughing and looked at me and said, 'Give this man indefinite leave!' And I said, 'Thank you, sir,' and went off thinking I'd won. Well, I think that the Regulating Petty Officer probably ran all the way back to his office, because I had hardly arrived home when I received a telegram instructing me to report to Belfast. I was being posted to a ship, the HMS *Dunvegan Castle*, and my war had really started.

HMS *Dunvegan Castle* was in Belfast docks, just finishing being re-fitted, when I arrived. She was an armed merchant cruiser and had been a large passenger liner, but built prepared for war with strengthening and gun mountings built into the ship, so that if war broke out one could put in gun emplacements very rapidly, and change her into a warship. She had eight six-inch guns and six four-inch guns, as well as anti-aircraft machine guns, but she was pretty useless really. Of the fifty-six-armed merchant cruisers that were sent out with convoys, I believe that fifty-two of them had been sunk by the end of the war. One of them, the *Jervis Bay*, you may have read or seen films about. She turned around and steamed straight towards a German pocket battleship, but of course she was sunk before her gun power could reach the battleship. The armed merchant cruisers were useful mainly as communication centres for convoys, but they couldn't really defend convoys, and they weren't fast enough. They weren't heavily enough armoured and they hadn't got anti-submarine capability. They could look after a convoy and give it instructions. They would relay information from the Admiralty when U-boat packs were known to be about, when they would instruct the whole convoy to zig-zag or speed up and they would generally shepherd the convoy, but that's all they could do really.

Anyway, we were in harbour in Belfast at Christmas in 1939 whilst the fitters were finishing work on the *Dunvegan Castle*. We were in the middle of our Christmas dinner when the First Lieutenant piped 'Clear the lower deck' which meant that everybody in the ship's company down below who was not an officer had to report up on deck to sweep snow off the decks after which the men went back to cold dinners. Nobody on the ship ever forgave him for that. He was not a popular man! He never became popular in any way. I was in a position to know that the Captain didn't think much of him either, because I had been appointed the Captain's Messenger. At first, I thought that being Captain's Messenger was a pretty lowly sort of job. I was then only an ordinary seaman on two shillings a day (when I became an able seaman I got three shillings a day). However, Captain Hubert Ardill RN was an excellent man, and it turned out to be a very good job. My duty was to be at the Captain's side and if he wanted anything done, I did it. When I had taken round his night order book I was free for the night, and I never had any night watches unless something happened and he needed me. I wasn't confined to any one part of the ship, I had no gun crew work to do, and I collected and had sight of all the confidential signals because I took them to him. So, for about a year I saw a great number of highly secret signals and I found my job very interesting.

I became part of a group of half a dozen RNVR people on board who were friends, and we had amongst us some interesting chaps, one of whom was a concert pianist. He was a sailor now of course and wore bell bottoms, but as a civilian he had actually been a concert pianist and when we went ashore at Greenock he played the piano in the canteen. Well, a lady had approached him and asked him if he would give a concert, and he had agreed. It turned out that she was the Admiral's daughter. The following evening, we all went ashore and went to a hotel for a drink. We were drinking Pimm's and at the next table were three or four young RNVR officers, and they started making fun of us among themselves. 'What are sailors doing drinking Pimm's?' and so forth. We overheard what they were saying, and they were being incredibly rude. Well, the big, wide doors swung open and in stepped a charming young lady who turned out to be the Admiral's daughter. The young officers leapt to their feet and moved around to offer her a seat and so forth and she said, 'Oh, no, thank you, I'm alright', and she walked straight past them and sat down next to Jimmy Green, the pianist who was going to play at the concert she was organising. Apparently, Jimmy had asked her to come along and join us for a drink, and the rude young officers slunk out of the room. It is perhaps not a very interesting story, but it was gratifying at the time.

Well, we were in the Clyde for orders with a launch streamed astern. We were only going to be there for a few days. We had been painted in grey and black camouflage for the North Atlantic, where we were bound to help the North Atlantic convoys, or so we thought, and it seemed obvious that this was going to happen pretty soon. Whilst we were waiting, a French cruiser came in and anchored a little way away. The captain of the cruiser had a motor launch streamed astern, held by its painter (that's the line with which one ties a small boat to a big ship) around the bow of the launch to the stern of the cruiser. Anyway, the Captain looked at this and said to me, 'Shannon, that French cruiser over there has a launch stream to stern.' 'Yes, sir?' I said. 'Well, we haven't got a launch. Do you think we could get it?' I said, 'Well, I'll try and find out, sir.' And I went to see the old Chief Bosun's mate and said, 'The Captain would like that Froggy's launch, because we haven't got a launch. Do you think we could get it?' He said, 'Well, yes, I should think so.' So, after dark the Chief Bosun's mate sent a boat across with muffled oars. It was the first time that I had seen muffled oars used (it's sacking around the oars so that they don't make any noise in the water), and they quietly rowed across in the dark and cut the painter, and then quietly towed the launch back to our ship. We hauled the launch on board, and we upped anchor and then we were away down the Clyde, heading off to the North Atlantic with the Frenchman's launch. We heard that it caused quite a stir when the French found that they had lost their launch, but nobody ever put two and two together or said anything to us about it. However, on our way down the Clyde we got a signal to say that our orders had been changed and that we were being sent to the South Atlantic. There was a change of plan, and we were going to escort convoys coming up from Freetown in Sierra Leone to Ushant off the coast of France, where we would hand them over and go back and pick up another convoy.

But there was a problem. We were going to the South Atlantic but we were camouflaged for the North Atlantic and so within twenty-four hours we had in effect to paint a huge passenger liner in the tropical camouflage colours of lavender, sand, grey and white. The men turned to with buckets of paint and whole handfuls of cotton waste with which you could cover square yards at a time, and they were lowered over the side on planks of wood and ropes to daub the sides, so that within twenty-four hours the *Dunvegan Castle* was transformed and we were on our way down to Freetown. The crew put away their dark blue suits and dark blue caps, and we were issued with white tropical kit that had been brought aboard secretly.

We called in at Dakar on the way, the capital of Senegal. We called in at Dakar in the early days to get oil, but later on we had to re-fuel at sea. When we had any time off, such as in Dakar or later on in Freetown, as Captain's messenger I was free to go ashore. At Freetown, we had to anchor two or three miles offshore as they had no real harbour, but going ashore there and seeing Sierra Leone I found very interesting. Not that we got to shore very much but if the Captain didn't want me, I was free. It was also interesting to go to Dakar, which was more-or-less the most western European settlement in West Africa, and in those days, they didn't treat the natives very well and it was an incredibly decadent place. Senegal was part of French territory overseas in those days, or *France Outre-Mer*. It only became independent from France in 1960. That's an interesting thing about France, they currently still have five territories around the world which they consider an integral part of France. These territories have French laws, they speak French, they vote for French members of Parliament and they are treated as much a part of France as the native soil of France.

For the next eight or nine months, we ploughed our way up-and-down going to and from Freetown until we got west of Finisterre where we handed the convoy over to ships which could really look after it, such as some destroyers and perhaps a cruiser, and then back we went. It was monotonous in the extreme but it was dangerous at times, and I'm afraid that we lost an awful lot of merchant ships to U-boats. As I have mentioned before, we acted as a communications centre for the convoys and picked up messages from the Admiralty. There was a constant stream of reports about where they thought the U-boats were, and we relayed these to the Commodore of the convoy telling him what he had to do and if there were any U-boats within the area, whether to zig-zag and what speed the convoy needed be at for operational purposes. Sometimes we were at full speed, sometimes we were just at slow, and that was our job really, seeing that the ships kept in station and kept apart properly.

On Sunday mornings, in naval vessels there are what are called 'Divisions', a sort of Church Service. Prayers are said and it was rather surprising to see the people who would say prayers during the war, under those circumstances, and mean them. Anyway, we were having divisions one Sunday and the Captain was just saying a prayer asking for safety for those at sea, and just as he said it the whole ship shuddered. We had been hit by a torpedo that didn't explode, but of course we rushed to action stations and we got away.

It was pretty horrifying at times and I saw some terrifying sights, such as seeing a tanker full of aviation fuel hit by a torpedo, it catching fire from stem to stern and seeing little figures running along the deck with the whole thing alight and men jumping into the water. You don't forget. I remember the worst thing that I experienced was having to sail past a small boat with men adrift at sea in it, who expected to be picked up and were waving to us. We were under orders not to stop and they couldn't be picked up and we sailed past, leaving them behind in the ocean, probably lost, and it was an awful thing to have to do. It doesn't leave your mind something like that, it's there forever.

Then on our way back from taking one particular convoy we were sailing happily along minding our own business when a huge battleship suddenly appeared over the horizon and we realised that it was the French battleship *Richelieu*, the most powerful battleship in the world at that time. We told the Admiralty and the Admiralty said, 'Follow her, and report where she goes.' The *Richelieu* had escaped from Toulon in 1940 and made her way down the west coast of Africa. The French Admiral Darlan was a Nazi sympathiser and would not let his ships come and join the Allies or disperse them to territories overseas' ports, telling the majority of the French fleet to gather at Oran in Algeria. The British fleet went in and sank the French fleet in Oran, and it is not written or spoken about much but it happened, you can look it up in the history books. I don't know the exact figures but thousands of French sailors were killed by the British in one afternoon. [28] They went in and shelled them at anchor and put them out of commission.

[28] The attack on Mers-el-Kébir took place on 3rd July 1940. The raid resulted in the death of 1297 French servicemen. See Wikipedia 'Attack on Mers-el - Kebir', *Wikipedia* en.m.wikipedia.org.

It was a terrifying thing to have to do, but you see, we were afraid that the French fleet was going to join the Germans.

Anyhow, we came across the *Richelieu* and told the Admiralty and followed her, and each morning and evening at dusk she swivelled her big guns round and pointed them at us, just to make sure we kept our distance. We were able to tell the Admiralty that the *Richelieu* went into Dakar, and since nobody knew what she would do or what France would do the Admiralty swung into action. Our aircraft carrier *Hermes* was positioned over the horizon out of sight but it sent a launch into Dakar full of men dressed as French sailors. Chug-chug-chug-chug they went into Dakar port, and chug-chug-chug right up astern of the *Richelieu*, the biggest battleship in the world. Then they tipped a few depth charges over the side of the launch and a few minutes later the depth charges blew her propellers and rudder off. As the *Richelieu* could not be repaired in Dakar she was out of action for the whole of the rest of the war, but she did actually take a part in operations because she used her guns to warn off General de Gaulle when he wanted to set up the Free French Government in Dakar. The Senegalese didn't want him, and the Richelieu defended them, so he turned away and went back to England.

Of course, we could no longer go into Dakar for oil after that but had to re-fuel at sea, which meant that we spent the second longest time at sea without coming into port of any ship in the British fleet during the first year of the war. At the time, we came across the *Richelieu* we were going to pick up a convoy, which we then later did, and then when we came up past France it was just as France was collapsing. You need to understand that there was an established passageway for convoys which was heavily defended, and when the convoy got nearer Europe we defended the port side and the French defended the starboard side. When France collapsed in 1940 they withdrew their sea patrols from the starboard side of the convoy route without any warning whatsoever and we lost twelve ocean-going ships in twenty-four hours. It was very difficult to forgive the French for that, but they were lost and there wasn't much we could do about it really except to hope we could just get the rest of them home. It was a pretty sad time, and I remember the Captain banging his fist on the rail of the bridge and saying, 'Well, we know where we are now. Those so-and-so French never were any so-and-so good. Now we know where we are!' And we did. We weren't in a very good place.

Strangely, life aboard the ship wasn't unhappy. I started teaching some classes voluntarily as a ship's schoolmaster, although in actual fact once we had started the school aboard HMS *Dunvegan Castle* I found that I was paid for it, under rates of pay that I believe were introduced by Charles II. I got nine pence a day in old money, which is not much more than tuppence a day today. Men who came to the school were mainly Royal Naval Volunteer Reserve ratings, but some of them were RNR officers in the Merchant Navy. This took place every day. It was entirely voluntary of course, but it was quite good fun. A bugler went around the ship blowing his bugle saying that it was time for school, and he was called the drummer. Men came along if they were free during the dog watch, if they were not actually on duty, being lookout or gun crew or something like that. The dog watch was between four o'clock in the afternoon and eight o'clock in the evening, when the men did their sewing and repairs or did their washing in a bucket, or wrote home, or when they opened their ditty boxes. A sailor had something called a ditty box, in which he kept ALL his belongings. The modern Navy is very different now of course, but the only place a sailor had in those days to put his personal belongings was his ditty box, which was locked and stored and got out during the dog watch when he was free.

I smoked a little while when I went into the Navy. Tobacco was so incredibly cheap that everybody smoked and for a while I smoked a pipe, but looking back on in I realise that I only did this because I felt that it looked good! I rather fancied myself, standing on the bridge with a curly pipe, but one day I leant over to call out to somebody, and opened my mouth, and the pipe dropped into the water and I never smoked again.

After the *Richelieu* and the fall of France, when we had spent that pretty long spell at sea we were given four days' leave from Belfast, but four days' leave from Belfast meant that you spent most of your time travelling and didn't really get any leave at all. I had four days to get down from Belfast to Essex in wartime travelling conditions, and then back again, and I didn't get much more than one full day at home. Anyway, in August 1940 after about eight or nine months of this work we were told that we were going into the Clyde for a few repairs. We left the convoy at Finisterre, as normal, and steamed on by ourselves until late one day on a calm, blue evening off the north-west coast of Ireland, when looking forward to our leave and beginning to think that we were nearly home, we were suddenly torpedoed. The torpedo did a lot of damage to the steering of the ship and we couldn't steer. The engines were still running so we could still move, but we started going around in a big circle. There was nothing we could do about it so we slowed down and went to action stations, but we couldn't see much. It got dark and I was on the bridge with the Captain, when after some long time we saw a blue streak coming towards us in the water. The blue streak of course was another torpedo, and as there was nothing we could do to get out of the way we all moved to the other side of the bridge away from where it was aiming and waited for it to hit, which it did. Some of the ship caught fire and the Captain gave orders to abandon ship.

I have in my possession a copy of part of the log book of the German U-boat Captain who torpedoed us. He wrote quite a bit about it, and chiefly his thoughts were why didn't we sink? He couldn't understand why we hadn't gone down. Well, the reason the HMS *Dunvegan Castle* wasn't sinking was pretty simple really. Being a passenger ship, she was mostly empty. I don't suppose we used much more than a third of the space available in the ship and the rest had been filled up as an experiment, with thousands of sealed oil drums that were down in the hold. I don't know if they used this experiment in other ships. It could only have been used in ships which had a lot of space. Normal naval ships couldn't hold them, but oil drums may have been put into other armed merchant cruisers. I really don't know, but these empty sealed oil drums acted as buoyancy aids and kept us afloat and the U-boat commander couldn't understand this. He says that we were firing our four-inch guns and getting too close for his liking and so he dived to get away and stayed under for another hour and three-quarters or something like that, but when he came up we were still afloat, although by that time it appeared that we were going to sink. Well, he sailed around and when we didn't sink he torpedoed us AGAIN and although we still didn't sink immediately we were listed over very severely. Abandoning ship was not an easy matter from the listing ship, but a lot of boats got away. I remember one particular man being blown forty or fifty feet into the air before landing in the water, but there were actually not as many casualties as I had thought and via the marvel of the internet I learnt fairly recently that we only lost about twenty-five men, and there were some wounded. I had thought that we'd lost many more than that. They were actually picked up, which I was very glad about.

Anyway, as the lifeboats were being filled the Captain told me to go aft and have a quick look around aft to see if anybody was still aboard, and he would go for'ard. He stomped off in his inimitable way whilst I trotted off aft and went below, where standing at the door of a magazine was a sailor with his gun, guarding it. I said, 'What are you doing here?' And he said, 'Well, it's my station, John. I can't leave here until I've handed the keys over to somebody.' I said 'Well, give them to me', and he gave them to me and I told him to get up on deck and get aboard a lifeboat. He chucked his gun down and off he ran, and I've still got those keys and Simon Mark keeps them as a little curio from the war. It says on them 'Dunvegan Castle 6' 'magazine aft'. After that I went up and reported all clear as far as I could see and then the Captain said, 'Just a minute, come into my cabin', and in his day cabin there was another cabin leading from it where I'd never been before. It contained a big safe. It was huge safe, and he went to open it and I thought he was going to get out a lot of confidential books or something like that. (Naval books are 'weighted'. They have lead covers, so that they will sink.) But he got out a bottle of whisky and a bottle of brandy and said, 'We might need those later on'. He gave them to me to take to a boat. We thought everybody had got onto the lifeboats and we were going to get aboard the last lifeboat ourselves when we heard a voice, and we turned to go back and have a look but the Captain said, 'You get aboard, Shannon, that's an order: get aboard!' Well, I had to obey his command so I got aboard and he said, 'Lower away.' You could lower a lifeboat from the inside, and we lowered it down into the water and he was left alone on board, and went off to investigate the voice. To cut a long story short he found two men, one of whom was injured, and they got away in a boat that had been jammed, and we picked them up later on, so luckily that ended happily.

As our lifeboat touched the water the U-boat commander decided to put yet another torpedo into our ship. We were on the starboard side and the ship was heeled over towards us. The U-boat commander aimed his torpedo into the port side and with the explosion there came the almightiest amount of water up in the air and down over the ship like a waterfall. It came down the deck of the ship and right onto the top of us, and it seemed to us (other people thought the same as me when I asked them afterwards) that there was no means of escape. I thought that we couldn't possibly survive, but after probably only ten or fifteen seconds, but what seemed like ages, our heads came out of the water and there we were still in the lifeboat. It was of course awash to the gunnels, but we were still afloat. The lifeboat turned out to have built-in buoyancy chambers, and one couldn't sink unless these buoyancy chambers were pierced. We bailed the water out and we pulled away from the vessel, eventually picking up the Captain and these other two men, and for a few hours we were just waiting because we knew that our wireless operator had got off a message and so we were pretty confident that someone would come and pick us up.[29]

The HMS *Dunvegan Castle* didn't sink for something like two or three hours. I think the main magazine blew up and broke its back in the end. The oil drums did keep it afloat for a long while though, and we were picked up five or so hours after we had abandoned ship by the HMS *Harvester*. The *Harvester* was

---

[29] The HMS Dunvegan Castle was sunk by U-46 (Engelbert Endrass) on 27th August 1940. 24 ratings and 3 officers were lost and 249 crew members (twelve of them wounded) were picked up and landed in Scotland. See 'HMS Dunvegan Castle', www.uboat.net

a corvette on convoy duties in the Western Approaches and she steamed away and landed us at Greenock, but of course by then it was eleven o'clock at night or something. It was after dark anyway, and there was no system in place at that time for dealing with survivors who arrived in the Clyde out of office hours!! We were just taken to a train station platform where we hung around. When the office headquarters were open during the day they could give any survivors new clothes, a bath, some food and generally speaking look after them, but when the office had closed there was nothing. A lot of our men were wearing very little clothing and were covered with oil and some of them were injured, but eventually an empty train came in and picked us all up and we spent the next twenty-four hours slowly wending our way down to Chatham, being shunted into sidings to allow ordinary trains go by, travelling through England. We had no food until some sandwiches were passed in through the train windows at Peterborough by the Women's Royal Voluntary Service, bless their hearts, and then when we got to London about eighteen hours later we had a meal. The Captain then said that he was leaving us, and he went straight off to lodge a complaint with the Admiralty. He borrowed a flying jacket, and he was dressed in a pair of flannels and a vest or something, with the flying jacket, but no cap. He said goodbye to me and thanked me for my work, which I thought was very gracious of him in the circumstances and then he said to me, 'I shall not get another command, you know,' and I said, 'I hope you will, sir.' Normally in the Navy if an officer loses his ship he finds it hard to get another command, but as it turned out he did get one. The Admiralty sacked the Admiral in charge of the Clyde straight away as a result of the lack of help we had had, and they set up a proper round the clock system for dealing with survivors. By an extraordinary coincidence my father, when he worked at the Naval Defence Office in the Clyde, was put in charge of this operation and he was of course very keen to do it. It really was a rather strange coincidence that he should get that job. I met him in Glasgow once, when he told me that he didn't really think that he was the man for the job and felt out of his depth. Just after this he went up in an aeroplane with a member of the Cabinet, an Admiral and a General who were debating the defence of the Clyde, and they asked his opinion but he said that he was not a trained staff officer and that his opinion would not be of any value to them. After they landed he resigned, saying that he wasn't suitable for the role. But he did a great deal more later on, and was assigned to the Headquarters of the Marines at Lympstone where he became Company Commander of 45 Commando, as I have already mentioned. He was an old-fashioned Marine officer, and I don't think that they come any better. When we were short of bomb disposal officers towards the end of the war, he trained as a bomb disposal officer and worked as one, to his eternal credit.

Well, once the remaining company of the *Dunvegan Castle* had got back to Chatham we were given leave. We got what was called Survivors' Leave. I went home, but apparently Lord Haw-Haw (the German propaganda ruffian) had mentioned on the wireless about our ship being sunk, and my aunt had heard this and told my mother.[30] I hadn't told my mother as I didn't want to worry her. I had just said that I'd got leave, and she was so angry with me that she wouldn't talk to me for the rest of my leave, which I thought was a little bit unfair.

Perhaps this is the time to insert the story of my, and Eileen's, wartime visit to my old college. I was on leave and petrol coupons were allowed to sailors on leave. This didn't amount to very much, but it was enough whilst the leave lasted and Eileen and I decided to go on a day trip to Winchester. We had a car which between us we had bought two or three months before the war. It wasn't much of a car. It cost £29 and it was garaged in a shed with a horse belonging to the delivery man of a local dairy. Anyway, we decided to go down to Winchester on a little jolly and we drove down, and driving through the college gates we entered the college grounds. We hadn't got very far, about forty or fifty yards or so, when out jumped an armed guard who refused to believe that we had come in through the gate, and couldn't imagine how we had got there without coming through the gate. We couldn't have come through the gate as there were sentries posted at the guard house. But the plain fact was that we had: we had just driven straight through, and nobody had stopped us. Well, they didn't believe us and

---

[30] Lord Haw-Haw was a nickname applied to the Second World War-era broadcaster William Joyce who made pro-German propaganda broadcasts that opened with *'Germany calling, Germany calling',* spoken in an affected upper-class English accent. See Wikipedia 'Lord Haw-Haw', *Wikipedia* en.m.wikipedia.org.

we were arrested. Their young officer demanded to inspect our papers. I told him that he could ring the Admiralty and check up on all my details if he wanted, but he wasn't impressed, and then it occurred to me that Mr Hull, the head groundsman, might still be about. I'd had a lot to do with him because of the tennis courts, whose upkeep we had discussed at least twice a week for a year. Luckily, he was still there and they got him and he recognised me from about thirty yards away, pointing towards the car. The officer said something to him and then he came over and said, 'Yes, he recognises you perfectly well.' I was therefore who I said I was, and could turn around and leave. I later learnt that the college was the headquarters of at least part of the Intelligence Corps and that somehow, we had driven through the gate without the sentries at the gatehouse noticing us.[31] I imagine that somebody suffered. That use was the last use we ever made of the car, because when the war ended and we had no means with which to run a car it was sold to a little local coal-merchant who cut the back off it, put planks on the chassis and used it to deliver coal around Barking!!

Back again in Chatham, I knew a little bit more about how things worked in the Navy this time and wasn't going to be caught again by the broom, as it were. On my first day back, I immediately applied to go to the naval school, to learn about

---

[31] From June 1940, the government had commandeered the college for military purposes. See Martial Rose, *A History of King Alfred's College Winchester 1840-1980* (London: Phillimore and Co., 1981) p. 90.

navigation and pilotage. I knew that there was a school on the barracks and that I might be able to go and do lessons there instead of doing ordinary duties, and I thought it would be interesting. I turned up, only to be informed on the second day, 'You needn't come back after today. Captain Ardill has recommended that you be trained for a commission.' I was taken aback, but looking back on it, I suppose, vaguely excited. I had no idea where it would lead. To this day I can remember the feeling of slight anxiety, coupled with some anticipation.

Chapter Six: Engaged to be married

When Eileen and I were in our forties we compared notes, and I was surprised to learn that neither of us had romantic dates with other people when we were younger. Through all our platonic friendship when I was away at college, deep down perhaps we knew that we were meant to be together. This became plain to me when we went to Whipsnade one day after I had left college. I had to work during part of that vacation too of course, but when we both had the day off we decided to go to the zoo. I was arranging the picnic and putting down the rug and getting out the grub, and there were some wallabies I recall, hopping around hoping to get some food. Eileen was looking at the camels. I've got a photograph of the back of her wearing a three-quarter length white jacket thing looking at them, just before she turned around and looked at me. I had just settled down on the rug and we stopped and looked at each other and in that second, we knew that we were more than just good friends. We continued as normal after going to the zoo, meeting up fairly often to play tennis, and Eileen also helped me with the play-leading I did in the run up to the war. Everybody knew it was coming, as I have said, and of course we knew that we would be parted as soon as war broke out because I had enlisted.

At that time there seemed to be two sorts of people, those who thought that ideas of marriage were silly, given the fact that a war is completely unpredictable and those who rushed into it because there was this element, unpredictability. We skirted around the subject. We were not engaged and I was away. By this time, Eileen and I had been completely inseparable, except when we were following our own considerable activities. Eileen started her air-raid precautions duties on top of her normal job. A few months later in 1940 when I got the four days' leave from Belfast from the *Dunvegan Castle* (which meant that I had only got less than two days actually at home in Barking), I asked Eileen if she would like a Jolly Jack Tar Brooch. Almost all the girls who had sailor friends wore Jolly Jack Tar Brooches, and she said that she would like one very much, and we went up to Ilford and in the short time we had spare we found a branch of Samuel's the Jewellers and went in to buy the Jolly Jack Tar Brooch. That's when I asked her, 'Wouldn't you really rather have a ring?' Well, she thought that it would be rather nice if she could have a ring, and so I stood blocking the expensive rings and she chose a ring that she liked, and then she said to me, 'Which finger do I put it on?' To this very day I am a bit ashamed that I never had the courage to ask her then if she would marry me outright. I lost my nerve at the very last minute. But I did tell her to put the ring on her engagement finger which she did, and within literally a few hours I was off back to sea, although now of course we had become engaged. *No bended knee, no appropriate words, no occasion or place. The scene has haunted me. Eileen would never have the ring changed for a decent one later on. It was buried with her.*

Well, we didn't see each other for a while. When Eileen lived with her grandmother she was not allowed to do anything in the house. She wasn't even allowed to make a cup of tea or to boil an egg which I feel must have been difficult. Her aunts and her grandmother thought that they had to watch over her and to their credit they did so, but it must have been very difficult for Eileen. After they evacuated and she was left alone to carry on during the war she had to learn to look after herself, and needless to say she managed perfectly well. At the time Eileen was working for the Civil Service in Ilford, and Barking, Ilford and East London were all pretty badly hit in the Blitz. After she had finished work Eileen used to regularly go up to my father's house and prepare some sort of meal for him. He was an ARP warden at the time and he had to get home from working in London, have a meal and go out for his ARP duties on most nights. Eileen came up to our house and made his meal, then went back to her house, and then either went down into the dug-out shelter or up to Ilford to her own ARP duties. It was not an easy life. For three nights a week she went up on top of the highest building in Ilford and relayed to the Fire Service exactly where the German bombs had dropped. But it didn't bother her, she was never afraid of anything, physical or psychological. *It was a bleak life. The Blitz was terrifying. Nightly bombing raids left people to crawl out of their air raid shelters, pull themselves together, sometimes climb over the rubble, and go off to work.*

Anyway, as I said, after I arrived back in Chatham after we had lost the *Dunvegan Castle* I was sent off to do officer training at Brighton for six weeks on the Captain's recommendation. The course was only for six weeks but it was six weeks of utter slog, and the one place where I went with the Navy where I genuinely had to work extremely hard. We had a very great deal to learn in six weeks, and each thing we learnt was tested. A lot of the stuff was never of much use but some of it was, and I believe that the course improved as the war went on. We worked from eight o'clock in the morning until about ten o'clock at night, with extra duties on Sundays at odd times, and at night we sometimes turned out for night duties. One night we had a look-out exercise on the beach. We were given a gun and lined up on the beach looking out to sea, about a yard or two apart with a rifle and a round each. We were to fire a shot if we saw anything untoward happening, such as a spy trying to land, when we were supposed to let off a shot to warn everybody. I was looking at my rifle, as I hadn't used rifles of that sort before and I was interested in how it worked, but in doing so I dropped my bullet in the sand. I'd lost it in the dark and I couldn't find it, and when the exercise was over I had to go back and tell the Chief Gunner's mate that I'd lost this bullet. I can remember the look on his face now, 'You've lost your bullet!?!' He was a big man, but I've never seen a man's neck and face expand so much as when he addressed me. He went red and then blue, and what he had to say to me was quite uncomplimentary, but it ended with, 'Get back on that beach and search all night until you find it!' Anyway, I had to go back and search for the rest of the night but I never found it.

We had to learn to signal by Morse code, by lamp and with flags, and Eileen used to come down from London at the weekends when most of our time together was spent with her testing me on all the stuff I'd been learning, although we had some nice moments together. There was a lot of information which I had to learn, and she liked testing me apparently. I enjoyed having her there, although I couldn't really get to see too much of her. *My friends on the course found her delightful and I was constantly reminded of what a fortunate man I was. I knew this, but the unanimous opinion of colleagues was very pleasant. They queued up to dance with her and as I remember they were all much better dancers than I would ever be. This was a special period of our time together, leading up, as it did, to our wedding.* Anyway, at the end of the course I was granted ten days' leave in order for us to get married.

When we got engaged we had agreed to get married when I next had leave. We hadn't known when that would be, so I was commissioned before we got married. To be given ten days' leave seemed impossible to contemplate. It was January 1941 and it was wonderful to be given ten days off after eighteen months in the Navy, but of course the Blitz was going on over London at the time. We didn't think that we should get married in Ilford, and decided to see if we could get married in North Cheriton, where I had been billeted with the Rector, and to ask the Rector if he would marry us. When he said that he would, Eileen sent a hat to North Cheriton and paid nine pence a week as rent for this hat to be lodged in a house in the village, as a condition of the Special Licence. The Rector was prepared to marry us with a Special Licence and he charged us none of the Church Fees, which was very good of him.

John and Eileen on their wedding day

We were married on January 26 1941, and the wedding took place on a Sunday morning during the normal village service. *It snowed during and after the wedding which took twenty minutes.* My brother Dan came down to play the organ but because of the Blitz few members of my family could get down from London and Eileen had none of her family there, because of the war, and because of her parents being in India. All told we only had seven guests, but Eileen had her old friend Doreen Baxter to be her bridesmaid, and Doreen's father came to give Eileen away. Doreen's brother came too to be the Usher. This was Raymond Baxter, who later became known nationally on the television and radio for *Tomorrow's World* and as a commentator at big, state occasions. He was about nineteen at the time and he was as excited as you could be to be an Usher at his sister's friend's wedding. He and his father cycled over forty hilly miles to get to the wedding, bless them.

I was resplendent in my brand new naval dress uniform wearing my dress sword. I was ignorant of customs. I remember the ignominy of getting to the church entrance and not knowing whether I had to take my sword off to go into church. I took the sword off and stood it in the umbrella stand. When we processed out, I had to get the sword out of the umbrella stand and buckle it on again and I felt like an idiot, and I discovered later that I should have worn it for the ceremony. *Eileen did not have a big wedding but she was satisfied with the nine people at her reception. She looked lovely and put on the SAME outfit for the private celebration with me of our Diamond Wedding. It still fitted beautifully. She made her own 'going away dress' and hat partly in the air raid shelter.*

After the wedding, we spent that night at the house of a Mr and Mrs Doe. Mr Doe was the head huntsman of the local lady of the manor, who owned a delightful house nearby and had two private packs of hounds, and we stayed with them overnight before making our way to the coast. We didn't mind where we went, but we wanted to go to the coast, and we eventually made our way to Lyme Regis. Transport in war time wasn't easy but we managed to take the train to Axminster where we found a bus that was going to Lyme Regis. We carried our cases from the station down to the front and walked along the promenade until we found *The Bay Hotel*, where we managed to get a room. All the windows looked out to sea, and we were right above the front door with a window overlooking the sea. We actually went back to the same room for our Diamond Wedding, and when the management compared hotel registers from 1941 and 2001 they then treated us like royalty. It was almost comical. The Chef came up to discuss with us exactly what we wanted for all our meals, and then the management managed to lose the bill.

It will be very difficult for most people nowadays to understand what a glorious feeling it was to have eight or nine days of peace and quiet ahead of us before we had to take up life at war again. Nine days of bliss, nine days in which to do what we liked and to forget all our problems and loneliness before we had to go back. I can remember the delight of settling into the hotel. Here we were. It is just impossible to describe the feeling. On the first night, it was pretty late I think, we went up to our room and had both just got into bed, when there was a noise on the promenade outside the window and then a crashing and banging of boots up the stairs, and then our door was broken in and into the room jumped soldiers pointing their guns at us. An officer followed and pointed his revolver at my head. 'Who are you?' he demanded, 'and who's that woman in bed with you?' I told him who I was and showed him my papers, and explained that Eileen was my wife and that I'd just got married and he said, 'A likely story. Stay there, don't move, don't attempt to get out of bed or to leave the room. There will be armed men in the room all night.' With that he went. Well, I can remember it as clearly as if it was yesterday, Eileen said to me, 'Is anything wrong?' I said, 'No, not really. It'll get sorted out.' I knew that there couldn't be anything really wrong. 'Oh, good,' she said and she turned over and went to sleep. She trusted that it would be alright. I didn't sleep so easily but I did get some sleep, and in the morning the young officer came back with my papers. They had looked into them overnight and realised that they had made a mistake. He said, 'Oh, it's alright, we checked you out, you can go now,' and he dismissed his men and turned to leave the room. I got on my high horse and summoning up all the dignity I could muster I said, 'Just a moment. You arrest an officer of His Majesty's Fleet and put him and his wife under armed guard all night, and then you tell us that we can go! I demand an explanation!' So, he explained to us that last night our blackout curtain had flapped when we had opened a window, and light had flickered from the room. There appeared to be signalling out to sea. A ship at sea had spotted this and reported that there was signalling going on from the hotel, and the local soldiery thought that they had caught a spy red-handed. They had been cock-a-hoop, obviously. So, I congratulated him on the speed of response of his men and he saluted smartly, very differently from before, and turned on his heel to walk out of the door. He had nearly left the room when he turned back and looking at me he smiled and said, 'You've got a very pretty wife, sir,' and quickly disappeared.

But we still had eight days of our honeymoon left. Eight days to do what we liked in. I can't really describe what it was like, having spent all that time at sea with very little leave and not seeing Eileen and the rest of the people I loved. The fact that we were at war didn't matter. The fact that in eight days' time I had got to go back and would be sent somewhere else didn't matter. After breakfast, we went out for a walk and the world was ours. We went up the promenade, and walked a long way along the front and I don't think that we even talked. We just strolled along the front and then back again in time for lunch, and when we came back at lunchtime, very peaceful and happy, there was a telegram waiting for me lying on the hall desk. I picked it up and opened it and it said, 'Report immediately to Southampton to join HMS *Quentin Roosevelt*'. We looked at the telegram. It was dreadful. But, orders were orders and we went upstairs and packed our bags and sadly walked away from the hotel carrying our large luggage. To prolong our time together Eileen decided that she would come to Southampton with me before she went back to the Blitz, and to getting my father's supper. *She was aghast at the vessel in which her newly found husband was to go to sea. She returned of course, and it was four months before we met again for a short leave. The ship was as bad as Eileen thought but eight months with the Belgians was an experience.*

However, it was at about this time that my father was recalled to the Marines, and he was like a dog with two tails. *When Eileen was married she had had to give up her post.* It was then arranged that Eileen should go down to Wincanton in Somerset, where my mother was helping to run a home for children who were maladjusted in the evacuation. This was voluntary work she was doing with a friend called Mrs Welling. They did a wonderful job with the children, some of whom had been to four or five houses where the host families couldn't cope with them.

Eileen found herself back in the small town where the reception after her wedding had taken place. This meant something to her and she was happy to work there 'living in'. I was able to stay there with her when I had leave and thus we had a few days just living together in the region where we were married, in the depths of the country. Eileen said that it must have been ordained.

My mother and Mrs Welling, and then Eileen, ran a home for about six or seven children, and most of the children became quite well adjusted. My mother eventually left Wincanton to join my father, but Eileen stayed on to run the home with Mrs Welling until our son John was about to be born. *Eileen loved the work there and learned a great deal about children with difficulties. It confirmed her belief that she should have been a teacher. Mrs Welling, with whom she worked was a very competent housewife, a very good cook and a pleasant person with absolutely expert skills in dressmaking. They fitted in well together. Eileen's gold medal in elocution was put to good use and story time in the hostel was awaited as was piano playing and singing. These children who gave trouble wherever they went, were generally pleasant and amenable in the hands of these two ladies and worked joyfully on the vegetable patch, which was a feature of the area. It was remarkable to see children who had been moved from school to school and half a dozen host homes and found too difficult to continue with, becoming reasonably amenable youngsters when dealt with by these ladies, who had no training.*

However, Eileen found that she was pregnant and obviously would have to give up the work. She then went to Exmouth where my mother was living at a house called *The Turret* on Hulham Road and stayed with her until she went into the Caroline Nursing Home for John to be born. *The nursing home was recommended by the doctor. It was not a good choice.* Eileen was there for three and a half weeks because of a physical problem at the birth, but I was more than forty years old before I knew this. She had simply never mentioned it; she never complained. John was born on June 22, 1942.

Chapter Seven: The Faroes

After being ordered to report to the HMS *Quentin Roosevelt* in January 1941, I made my way to Southampton docks where I found a dreadfully ugly-looking ship which turned out to be an ex-French fishery protection vessel, the FPV *Flamant*.[32] When France collapsed this ship had been in one of our ports, and we had taken it over and decided to re-fit it and make it into an anti-submarine patrol vessel. At that time, there were quite a number of Belgians in England who had escaped from the continent and wanted to join the British Navy, and so the Navy decided to make them into a Naval Section all of their own. This French ship, re-fitted, was handed over to them as the HMS *Quentin Roosevelt*, the first ship of the Royal Navy Section Belge. The crew were all Belgians, and the Admiralty was looking for an officer who could speak French and in its wisdom, they sent me. In those days, I could speak French reasonably well, and as I hadn't got a job at the time this task fell to me. Unfortunately, I quickly found out that the men on board were all Flemish and had no time for the Walloons, the French Belgians. In fact, they detested the Walloons, and wouldn't allow French to be spoken aboard ship under any circumstance. However, the idea was for them to learn English and a lot of them knew quite a deal of English already because many were fishermen and had traded with English fishermen most of their lives. As part of my job I liaised with Mrs Hastings-Orde, who was known as *La Fée des Belges* (the fairy-

---

[32] The ship had been re-named after the son of President Roosevelt.

godmother of the Belgians), and who distributed amenities to the Belgians in Britain.

The Captain of the HMS *Quentin Roosevelt* was called Frank Allen, and he was an RNR officer and the youngest extra-master mariner in the whole of the British merchant fleet. He was an excellent seaman to whom I owe a great deal. I learnt a lot from him, and without his help at the beginning I doubt whether my time as an officer would have been as pleasant and as satisfying as it turned out to be. Shortly after I joined the ship the First Lieutenant fell ill and was invalided out, and Frank signalled the Admiralty and asked for permission to appoint me as First Lieutenant in his place. I had got on very well with the Belgians during our initial training, and I got on well with Frank and he wanted me as his Number One. The Admiralty agreed even though there were two officers on board who were senior to me. This was rather unusual, and I doubt it had ever happened before, but it was wartime and these were unusual circumstances. I spent the whole of HMS *Quentin Roosevelt's* commission as the First Lieutenant and it actually worked well. The other two officers were happy with the idea, and in fact I think that neither of them had wanted the job as they didn't want the bother or the effort of organising a ship's company. The First Lieutenant looks after the running of the ship, he organises the Watches and that sort of thing and he is also in charge if the captain is away. I liked it actually: I got on well with my fellow officers and I was quite happy to be made Number One.

We were in dock in Southampton being re-fitted when a German bomb dropped right through the funnel, making a hole in it and landing on the quay side. The ship had a huge funnel and so the bomb did very little damage and didn't explode, thank goodness. We collected the nose cone of the bomb and mounted it in the wardroom, and when the ship was decommissioned we were going to draw lots for someone to take the nose cone home. Nobody wanted the heavy great lump of metal in the end as it was too big and heavy. As the HMS *Quentin Roosevelt* was being re-fitted we set to sorting things out, preparatory to proper training of the ship's company. Frank told the fitters that the ship was too top-heavy because they had installed guns and depth charges and concrete slabs right round the bridge. But the fitters, who were from Camper Nicholsons, came aboard and they said that it wasn't.[33] Frank insisted that it was, but he was overruled and the Admiralty ordered us off to Tobermory, on the Isle of Mull, for three weeks, where in Navy parlance we were going to be 'worked up'.

Leaving Southampton, we had a signal to help take a convoy through the Channel, and we reported to the Commodore of the convoy and took up our place. It was my turn to take the

---

[33] Camper and Nicholsons are the oldest leisure marine company in the world. Like many commercial companies with skills vital to the war effort, they were taken over by the British Government at the outset of the war. See Wikipedia 'Camper and Nicholsons' wikipedia en.m.wikipedia.org.

watch in the middle of the night and Frank, knowing that he had a green, young officer who had never stood on a bridge alone in his life, treated me as if I was an old hand and said, 'Keep on the port quarter of the Commodore and let me know if anything happens. If you want me, I'll be in my night cabin.' However, I'm sure that he didn't go to sleep. He sat up in a chair with his ear to the door I imagine, waiting and listening. Well, as you might expect the convoy was attacked and we heard the German bombers coming over and dropping bombs over the convoy. Luckily no damage was done, nobody was hurt and we didn't actually have to go into action, although in the morning the convoy had rather got out of formation. Later that morning we broke away from the convoy and proceeded north to Tobermory. We stopped on the way at Milford Haven to have a tiny bit of damage attended to, and then for some reason which escapes me, we stopped again at Holyhead, and were approaching when we got a signal saying, 'Do you know that you are in a minefield?' They had laid a minefield and somehow, we had not had notice of it, whereas normally notice of this sort of thing came through to every ship. Nowadays of course such news would come via IT in some way, but in those days, we had what were called 'Admiralty Fleet Orders' that were sent to all ships. I can only presume that we must have left Southampton before we got the latest updated orders and so we had to admit that no, we didn't know that we were in the middle of a minefield. Then, straight ahead of us, someone reported a mine floating on the surface. Frank manoeuvred the ship very skilfully, and ordered men to lean over the side of the ship with oars and to just gently push the mine away as we edged forward, until in the end it disappeared astern and all was safe. I don't think that there was ever any serious danger; it was just part and parcel of being at war.

We then arrived at Tobermory where we met the Flag Officer in charge, Commodore 'Stephen' Stephenson, a very fiery man whose personal assistant was a man named Richard Baker (who later became a newsreader on the Television and Radio and also always used to introduce the promenade concerts). The idea was that for three weeks the Tobermory staff would train the ship's company but they didn't get very far because of the Belgian language problem, and Commodore Stephenson got rather fed up with us and cut our training short. But before this he tried to test us a bit. He sent a boarding party in the middle of the night to see if we were awake, but we were on the alert and the Belgians, who were a little wild, repulsed the boarding party quite seriously with meat cleavers and all sorts of improvised weaponry. Well, the Commodore didn't think much of this so the next night he sent a party across to steal our dinghy which was streamed astern, and later I thought of the French one that we'd stolen. He managed to get our dinghy without our look-outs noticing, for which Frank was called over and hauled over the coals. He came back from this dressing-down and vented his wrath upon the men, so that the following night without our knowledge they went across and stole the Commodore's launch, which wasn't received in a very kindly light. This type of test was sprung on all ships under training, at any time. Our engineers were working on our motorboat, as there was something wrong with the gears (it wouldn't go forward, it could only reverse), when they got a signal to take the Commodore ashore from his flag ship. They went across to pick him up stern first, and took him ashore, and he didn't think much of that either. However, if you ever go to Tobermory and go to the museum you will find a description of our time in that port being 'worked up'. It is quite interesting in its way. There has recently been a beer brewed called 'The Terror of Tobermory', in honour of Vice-Admiral Sir Gilbert Stephenson.

Eventually we got a signal to proceed to Scapa Flow in the Orkneys to report to the Flag Officer in charge of the Orkneys and Shetlands, Admiral the Earl of Cork and Orrery. When we arrived at Scapa Flow we were the only ship there belonging to a friendly foreign power, and we were flying both the white ensign and the Belgian flag which meant that the Admiral, observing protocol, had to come out to us with all his retinue. Normally of course the Captain would have had to go ashore and make his number to the Flag Officer in charge. Well, I would guess that the Admiral stayed aboard less than three minutes, and he had only been back ashore for a minute when we got a signal, 'Proceed to the Faroes for a period of duty.' They were getting rid of us.

Kirkwall is the largest town in the Orkneys. We were to be a member of the Kirkwall anti-U-boat flotilla but we would be based in the Faroes, where neutral shipping had to be vetted. People forget that at any given time there was an enormous number of neutral shipping on the oceans during the war.

Neutral ships weren't attacked but they had to be controlled, and all shipping coming across the North Atlantic had to come down through the islands of the Faroes to be checked and examined. We had to make a note of their codes, and they had to be able to give us sundry details which they had been given when they left their home port. Neutral ships regularly left the Americas and sailed across the North Atlantic during the war, plying their trade right into the Baltic without any interference from the German U-boats, and they were lit up at night but they weren't attacked. Our job was to check these vessels, and also of course to perform anti-submarine patrols around the Faroes. Another job we had to do was to give permission to the Walrus aircraft to land. The Walrus was a British single-engine amphibious biplane reconnaissance aircraft that could only land on water, and we had to decide whether the water was sufficiently smooth for it to land. There was no area of land flat enough to make a landing strip on the Faroe Islands, so we would look at the weather and study the sea conditions, and then signal up to the pilot to say whether he could or could not land. If he couldn't land he went back to Aberdeen. I believe that our Engineers later improvised a landing strip. After the Americans moved onto the Faroe Islands at the time of the Second Front, they had only been there for about twenty-four hours when they started blasting out the side of a mountain to get a flat enough strip of ground on which to land aeroplanes.

Whilst we were based in the Faroes we would come down to Kirkwall occasionally, or go down to Aberdeen and back on different duties. We towed sea targets for the coastal batteries to have gunnery practice once, when one of these batteries was aiming at us rather than the target, and I was sent ashore to sort out the battery commander. I went into their office and putting on my best manner I asked for an explanation of their gunnery, only to discover sitting behind the desk one of my old college friends, Harold Watts. Watt-o, as he was called. He hadn't become a teacher but had gone into the Temple Choir and now here he was sitting in a battery office on the north-east coast of Scotland. He was in the Temple Choir all his working life, and taught singing as well.[34] Anyway, we got so involved in talking about old times and old friends that I forgot all about the wretched battery and their gunnery and what I had come for, so much so that when I got back to the ship I had to tell Frank that they had had something wrong with their calibration and that they were putting it right.

The Germans attacked light ships, or lighthouse ships. It was the first time in history that this had happened, and so these had to be serviced fairly frequently but then the Germans started attacking the service vessels. The *Northern Lights* service vessel therefore had to be escorted and we used to escort it to outlying coastal garrisons when I discovered that the Captain of *Northern Lights* was called Galbraith, and was a distant relative of Eileen. We also took the author Eric Linklater to some of the northern garrisons at this time, and he wrote his

---

[34] The Temple Church was built by the Knights Templar. The Round Church was consecrated in 1185. The Temple Church continues to resound to music. See, The Temple Church London www.templechurch.com.

book *The Northern Garrisons* for the Central Office of Information partly in my cabin.

Around that time, we helped to fight a fire that took hold of the *Mathilde Thorsen*. The *Mathilde Thorsen* was a brand new, neutral Swedish merchant ship, carrying grain and passengers, and it was her maiden voyage. She was a big ship and incredibly valuable, worth millions of pounds. This happened near Tórshavn, the capital of the Faroe Islands, and we tied up alongside and used our ship's pumps to help put the flames out. Being an ignorant landlubber, I wanted to put a shell in her sides to let water in to quench the fire but Frank stopped me, explaining that the grain would swell and burst the ship's hull. I remember saying to him, 'Not a bad thing: she's probably carrying hidden ball-bearings to the Germans'. For the record, at any time in history up to that point we would have been paid prize money for helping to save that ship, and I would have been quite wealthy because a percentage of the value of the ship would have been paid to me. This happened up until the First World War, but the practice was then stopped. My father got a small amount of prize money from his time with the Marines in the First World War but it was shared out on a vastly unfair system. The senior ranks got the lion's share of the prize money with about half to the captain and a quarter to the other officers, and the rest was then divided between the sailors. So, had things been different I would have certainly been given a very large sum of money, and as a family we would have been comparatively wealthy for the rest of our lives.

Another time when we were stationed in the Faroes, we had a signal from the Admiralty to say that there was a U-boat hiding between two of the islands. We couldn't find it, and in actual fact we didn't think that there was a U-boat there at all so Frank signalled the Admiralty to say that we had done our stuff and that we didn't think that there was a U-boat. We got a signal back telling us in no uncertain terms that it was there. I don't know what intelligence they'd had but they told us exactly where the U-boat was hiding and told us that we were to go back and plaster it with depth charges. So, we did as we were told and dropped the charges in the appropriate place but we honestly had no evidence that we had hit anything at all. Our Asdic detection equipment didn't pick up good echoes.[35] However, the Admiralty insisted that there was a U-boat there. One thing I can say is that whilst we were doing all this was there was an absolutely electric air aboard ship. The Belgians were absolutely alight. They were hitting back. Most of these men had families who were suffering in Belgium, and they had some pretty sad tales to tell. One man called Lafère had set off from Belgium in a boat with seven members of his family, and they had been machine-gunned on the way over and he was the only one left alive. So, the atmosphere was pretty electric. They were getting their own back.

At that time, I first met Lord Rowallen, Colonel of the Lovat Scouts, who were training in the Faroes. He used to come aboard for a drink each time we were in port. The Lovat Scouts

---

[35] ASDIC was an early form of sonar used to detect submarines.

were a Scottish Highland Yeomanry Unit. Later on, when I was stationed at Loch Ewe and Eileen had moved up to the cottage at Poolewe, Lord Rowallen had his headquarters just up the track from us in what is now a hotel called Pool House and he used to train his men around our cottage. But to meet him in the Faroes and then again on the mainland, was quite a coincidence. The Lovat Scouts went on to liberate the first house in France after D-Day. Much later after the war when Eileen and I were in France visiting the Café Gondrée, which is now a museum, I started speaking to a lady standing alongside me. As I was speaking to her I saw quite a large photograph on the wall and I said, 'I know that man. That's Lord Rowallen.' The lady smiled and said, 'Yes, I am Arlette.' Arlette was the little girl who let Lord Rowallen into the house when he and his men first arrived, and when we met her she must have been about fifty or sixty I suppose. I have a photograph that she signed for me.

Now the HMS *Quentin Roosevelt* was a pig of a ship and an uncomfortable one at the best of times. As I said previously, when it had been refitted Camper Nicholson's had put a lot of armour around the bridge. We had our depth charge throwers and light anti-aircraft guns and other things like that, and not only did the ship look ugly but according to Frank it was top-heavy. He had claimed it was top-heavy, but the fitters had said that it wasn't and we were sent off to war. Well, in bad weather she wasn't a very nice ship to be in; in fact, she was frightening. One day, Frank was ashore seeing the Naval Officer in Charge and he talked him into coming out for something or other from the Faroe Islands. I don't know what the pretext was but he got him to come out to the ship, and then he saw to it that we went across the swell and abeam of the sea and the waves, and the *Quentin Roosevelt* rocked and rolled. Every time she rolled over you thought that she wasn't going to come back, and the NOIC said, 'I don't like the feel of this ship at all.' 'No,' said Frank, 'she's unstable. We've been in the North Atlantic for eight months and I insisted that she was top-heavy before we started.' Anyway, the upshot of this was that the NOIC signalled the Admiralty and we were immediately sent down to Aberdeen to be tilted. You 'tilt' a ship to see if it's top-heavy and to measure its stability. Well, they measured this and of course she was top-heavy and they said, 'She's unstable. She'll have to come out of service, she's not seaworthy.' We had been tossing around in the North Atlantic for eight or nine months in this thing, but after this she was taken out of service immediately.

Well, that left us with the problem of what to do next. The Belgian authorities offered the ship's five British officers the 'Légion d'Honneur' if we would stay with the Section Belge; which now numbered quite a number of ships and ended up totalling twenty-nine. But we wanted to serve on British ships and we told them that we would rather do this. They accepted. The Belgians went on to take part in the Russian convoys and acquitted themselves very well, and they also began to specialise in mine-sweeping and they have become possibly the world's experts in mine-sweeping. We called upon them when we went to the Gulf War, to sweep for our ships. I'm really rather pleased about that. A few years ago, in 2012, I was asked over to Belgium as the only known surviving member of the HMS *Quentin Roosevelt*, the very first ship in the Royal Navy Section Belge, and I was given the very great honour of opening their new naval base, on the formation of 'The Belgian Navy'! [36]

HMS Quentin Roosevelt painted by John in 2013

[36] The new base is in Zeebrugge

Chapter Eight: Loch Ewe

After HMS *Quentin Roosevelt* was decommissioned towards the end of 1941 I went home on leave to Wilmington Gardens in Barking. I was very pleased to be home, but on the second day of my leave I was shaving upstairs and had actually just shaved one side of my face when there was a ring at the door, and Ronald Last the County Physical Education Chief for Essex was there with an envelope in his hand. I was fairly surprised to see him but I asked him in, half-shaven, and offered him a drink and we had a chat and then he said, 'I've got something to offer you. We've had permission from the Admiralty to offer you release from the Navy if you wish, to start up a Youth Service for Essex.' This was a new venture and quite an exciting one in its way, so I asked him what it entailed and he was just explaining it to me when there was another ring at the door. It was a telegram boy with a telegram for me which I opened, and in the telegram, was the offer of a command of one of His Majesty's ships. It was a very unimportant ship of course, but I was young and didn't give a second thought to organising the Essex Youth Service after the prestigious offer of the command of a small warship. I told Mr Last, 'I'm sorry, but I will be accepting the offer from the Navy.' He was very courteous about it and he knew there was no contest; so that's how I came to have my first command.

Commanding a ship is a job that very, very few people get to do and a job that most people would give a lot to do, and I found it very interesting. I spent the rest of the war in command of one vessel or another, none of them of very much importance but they were vessels that did some quite interesting jobs. 'Interesting' is a funny word to use about war, but I think it's true; they were all happy ships (considering there was a war on) and they were ships that went on some interesting operations.[37] I had to join my first command at Oban in the autumn of 1941, and Eileen was able to come up with me to Oban for two days just for the weekend. (Whilst we were there we bought a rug that Simon Mark's got now. It's a rug that was used for picnics throughout our lives and it is a bit the worse for wear now, but it holds many memories.) My command was a scruffy old vessel called HMS *Fairweather*, a small converted trawler with only two officers and a very good crew. She was not very nice looking but a good sea vessel, and we learned that we were to go up to the Minches off the north-west coast of Scotland. The Minches are sea straits between the north-west highlands of Scotland and the Hebrides, and we were to be based at Aultbea on Loch Ewe.

Into Loch Ewe came pretty well all the ships that had crossed the Atlantic from the Americas, and most of those that were going to re-cross the Atlantic came there first before they returned. It was the convoy gathering point for pretty well the whole of the British Isles at that time. Loch Ewe is a big sea loch with an island in the centre, and when we got there we

---

[37] John has advised us that: 'I admit to considerable pleasure when I once received a 'flimsy' from the base Captain, stating, 'that Whenever Lieutenant Shannon's ship is visited, the ship's company seem of a higher level than they can be''.

found a fairly large naval base: a temporary set-up with huts and a large amount of barbed wire. The Navy had put a boom right across the entrance to the loch (which was quite narrow) with electronic devices on the floor of the ocean outside the boom. There was a gate in the middle of the boom which was opened by two ships that were moored in permanent position at the entrance. They pulled back chains to let ships in and shut the gate immediately after the ship had passed. Before I arrived, they had had trouble with a U-boat getting in at one time, but the loch was a pretty safe harbour really.

The loch was getting very busy with merchant shipping and our first duties were in the Minches examining merchant ships going into Loch Ewe, and outside on anti-submarine patrol defending the loch. We carried a small number of depth charges. We had no Asdic, the early form of sonar used to detect submarines, but we had our wireless and we patrolled up and down outside Loch Ewe examining vessels as instructed. It could be a really boring job sailing up and down outside the loch and only coming in off patrol about every ten days for a couple of days to get stores and to take on fuel. All the way around the shore and in the hills roundabout were anti-aircraft guns, but it was really a bit too far for the German planes to fly to. German bombers needed to fly right across the North Sea and then right across Scotland to reach Loch Ewe, so as they were at the limit of their range when they arrived and couldn't stay long without refuelling they really didn't trouble us much at all. But we were ready for them. There was quite a big Army presence up in the hills with anti-aircraft guns, and there was also an RAF station not terribly far away; but the German planes didn't bother us. As far as I know, only once during the war did any plane drop anything, and that was one plane and it wasn't a very heavy bombing. The need for an anti-submarine patrol also diminished as the war went on when it became quite clear that the German U-boat fleet couldn't get right round the north coast of Britain and into the Minches very easily, and that ships were actually quite safe there. That's why Loch Ewe had been chosen, for its inaccessible position as well as its size.

But there was one problem, and that was the number of ships and convoys coming into Loch Ewe. The shipping traffic coming across the Atlantic was growing all the time. By 1943 material began to pour across in the build up to the second front, and the Navy couldn't cope with all the ships that needed to come into Loch Ewe as they couldn't provide a pilot service for them all. When a Merchant Navy captain gets near shore he gets very jittery, and the thought of having to bring a big ship through a little gateway and then into a narrow loch and anchoring it safely among other ships was really too much for them. Legally these ships had to have a pilot and the Navy had to do something about it and fairly urgently too, so they worked out a scheme which as far as I know was completely illegal under maritime law. Most Merchant Navy captains would not have subscribed to it had they known what was happening, I am sure. They were lied to in a sense. What happened was that the HMS *Fairweather* and other small craft were formed into two halves of a flotilla. We were told to use pilot lights at night and a pilot flag in the daytime which said to any ship coming in, 'There is pilot aboard, and the pilot will give you instructions'. A collection of young RNVR officers like myself were drafted in and given the job of instructing merchant ships without actually boarding them, and then of bringing them into the loch and actually escorting them right to the spot where they were to let go the anchor. Now this wasn't a very exciting job, but it was a responsible one. We had to pick up the vessel out in the Minches and then tell it very carefully exactly what it was to do: what the weather was like inside the loch, what the winds were doing, what the visibility was like and how far it had got to go to anchor, how much cable to veer out and what the characteristics of the sea bed were like where he was anchoring. The ships' captains had to follow our instructions exactly, they were told what speed to use and when to slow down, but right up until the moment when they let down their anchors they thought that they were being directed by a professional pilot. They never knew it, but they were putting themselves in the hands of young and relatively inexperienced British naval officers, and they didn't know it. We were no more pilots than they were. We knew the loch of course, very thoroughly, which is all that you needed to know really, and with no real experience we brought in these great ships that had battled their way across the Atlantic fully laden and it worked. That's the surprising thing about it. It worked.

When you had a whole convoy coming in and perhaps one also about to go out, the number of ships you could have in the loch was incredible. To people not used to it, it looked as if ships must collide with one another all the time as they swung round at anchor. The loch could take up to over a hundred ships, when it looked as if one could jump from deck to deck, although one couldn't of course. We had put them there, and we knew exactly the spots where they could be anchored. If you were used to it and you knew what was happening, it was quite safe. After the war I actually applied for pilotage money. I learnt that one could get this, and as I had piloted naval ships into most of the ports of the United Kingdom I wrote to My Lords at the Admiralty to see if I could get it. Every little helps. Anyway, I got it. I got back a long letter in flowery language from My Lords which I wish that I had kept, and roughly speaking, it said that they were pleased to pay me this certain sum of money at the rates that were laid down. Unluckily for me these were the same rates laid down in Charles II's reign, and my total for the work I'd submitted came to sixteen shillings and ten pence. (Incidentally, it was King Charles II who also gave the Navy it's prayer book, and the Church of England's Book of Common Prayer is based on that book.)

The best ships for the job of piloting were small craft that were fairly nimble and fairly fast, and motor yachts were ideal. There were some big, former luxury motor yachts at Loch Ewe that had been literally gin palaces in their former incarnation but they could do the job very well. They were fast and easily manoeuvrable and they were of course superb ships to be on and to live in. I realised this of course, and when the commanding officer of one of these yachts, the HMS *Aelda*, was sent on another job. I applied for a transfer from *Fairweather*, but to carry on working in the flotilla. This was granted and I went across and took over *Aelda*. She was a beautiful, big motor yacht, a luxury dwelling and a lovely ship, with big twin-engines. I thought that all my Christmases had come at once: *Aelda* was clean and it had gold-plated taps, wonderful blankets, and a beautiful ward room. (Some of these craft had things like silver cutlery that had been left aboard by their owners.) *Aelda* had light anti-aircraft guns and depth charges but no great armament, but she was a beautiful ship. We were getting one convoy in and another convoy out one night, and were chasing around at high speed when a large harbour service vessel with a steel hull suddenly crashed into her side. I had only been on *Aelda* a few weeks. There was a lot of activity in the loch that night, and to cut a long story short we were hit amidships by this vessel going at full speed and we sunk very quickly, and I'm very sad to say that some men were drowned. One of the saddest memories of my life is of my coxswain standing on *Aelda*'s deck after I had given orders to abandon ship saying 'I can't swim', and unfortunately, he was lost.

For my part I remember trying to swim and finding it rather difficult until I realised that I'd got my sea boots on. I managed to kick these off but it was difficult swimming in my uniform battle jacket and trousers. I found that I couldn't get them off in the water as I wasn't a competent enough swimmer. I was able to swim across to another ship in the flotilla, *Silver Cloud*, whose commanding officer was Claud Ramsey, a very great friend of mine and a friend of Eileen's. (We stayed with him after the war with our children, although they won't remember him.) But I had a fair distance to go, further than I had ever swum before, and I decided to do it in little stages, treading water and then going on again, keeping in mind the fact that I was swimming home. That way I covered the distance and climbed aboard at about ten o'clock at night, and I told Claud what had happened. He was a true friend and when I asked him to, he searched for <u>hours</u> for survivors. Eventually he returned and coming below decks he said, 'I don't think there is any chance of finding anybody else, John.' That must have been at about two o'clock or three o'clock in the morning, and when I said, 'Go on, Claud, go on until it's light', he just said 'Okay' and turned around and went back up and they searched until it was light. He was a good friend. I have been so lucky in having so many good friends. Oddly enough, a year or so later a barricoe (or water cask) from a lifeboat of the *Aelda* was washed up on the shores of Loch Ewe, and this was later given to us and it has been restored and lives in the hall in my daughter's house today.

I was given another ship, but because there had been loss of life there had to be a Board of Enquiry. It would have been a court martial in peacetime. It was not a good experience but at the end of the Enquiry I was thankfully exonerated from any guilt in the matter and I went back to work feeling a bit happier that it was all over, only to find a month or two later that the Admiralty were demanding that the Board of Enquiry be held all over again because they were dissatisfied that they had not apportioned blame on a percentage basis. So, the court had to be reconvened and they called back all the people who had sat on the original Enquiry, who were all over the world by now, to sit in the same room and go over the same ground six months later. It was a very uncomfortable period of our lives whilst we were waiting for this to happen. Fortunately for us I was again exonerated one hundred percent, but to this day I don't really think that anybody, in any kind of accident like that, can be exonerated totally. I met the skipper of the harbour service vessel about two years later, and he had obviously suffered very severely from having been given all the blame for the collision, and looked to have aged ten years. I had a long talk with him and strangely he appeared to alter visibly during our evening's conversation. As I was leaving he said that he was very glad that he had met me, because all this time he had felt that I had thought badly of him, and blamed him for the fact that some of my men had been lost. It had preyed on his mind, but I was able to reassure him that I looked on it as just an accident that happened at sea, and that although the Board of Enquiry had decided that I wasn't to blame it didn't mean that he held *all* the blame. I was quite sure that in any accident like that nobody could be one hundred percent to blame. All the Court meant was that as far as the Admiralty was concerned I wasn't to blame; they didn't say that he was to blame. A lot of blame was due to the conditions, the dark, the rain, the horrible conditions with ships darting all over the place signalling and flashing, ships going one way, ships going another way and there happened to be an accident. That certainly seemed to take a load off his mind and he was very grateful. He said that our meeting had made quite a difference to him and I was very pleased about that.

Normally I would not have got another ship, but the Captain of the base signalled to the Admiralty and said that he wanted to keep me in view of my knowledge of the base and of this particular piloting operation. I suppose that I had a good grasp of the job by then, and it wasn't a job that you could learn in five minutes and we were getting very busy. The flotilla was made up of about ten or twelve vessels and it was night and day work. You didn't have to be very clever but if you really knew the job you could do it, without being any great seaman or great harbourmaster. The Admiralty agreed and I was put aboard the *Jacana*, another luxury yacht that had come up from the Clyde to replace *Aelda*. As it turned out she wasn't terribly suitable for the job, as she was a bit too light. One had some very bad weather coming right down into the loch off the Minches, and when one felt the full force of the North Atlantic in winter it could be pretty terrible, and she was just a little bit too light for the job. But she was a very beautiful ship, very beautiful. The Commanding Officer who came up in her was sent somewhere else for another job, and he wasn't very happy about it. He was a chap called Silver, and the oldest son and manager of Silver's yachting boatyard on the Clyde, one of the country's two or three top boatyards for building and repairing yachts. As a matter of fact, in the end he became very friendly for the day or two that we were changing over and he left me the loan of an international 14-foot racing yacht. But I never used it much and didn't bother taking up yachting. At one time, there was a race organised around the island in the middle of the loch, Ewe Island. That was the only bit of proper sailing in small boats I ever did. Boats, dinghies and other small craft from most of the ships were taking part in this race, and I decided that we should have a go. We launched the dinghy and I set off, but I never actually got across the starting line and still hadn't crossed it when the race was nearly over, and so I went back to my vessel, and I never did any more dinghy sailing: I wasn't very good at it!

Pretty soon I asked to come off *Jacana*. I didn't think that she was suitable, and luckily, I was told that I could go back to *Fairweather*, which was also not exactly suitable for the job but more than capable of standing up to any weather we had. Before I did that I had to go and look after a ship called HMS *Dale Castle* for a month or two. HMS *Dale Castle* was being taken out of service because she was very old and clumsy and in need of repair, and I looked after her in the loch. We didn't go to sea. She was a very old converted trawler which amongst other things had been used at the beginning of the First World War for Winston Churchill to review the Minesweeping Fleet. I found a description of this on board, along with the whistle that had been used to pipe Churchill aboard and to pipe him off the ship. It wasn't a bosun's whistle (a bosun's 'call' is the proper name), but was just an ordinary whistle with 1914 stamped on it, and Simon Mark has that whistle now. Anyway, they had decided that the *Dale Castle* was too old and she was going to be broken up, and after I had looked after her for a month or two she was taken out of commission and I went back to the *Fairweather*.

In *Fairweather* my crew and I went back to the duty of piloting shipping in and out of the loch, which is when I witnessed the only accidental damage to merchant shipping in the whole three years I was on the loch. As far as I know we only had this one accident, because after all, we did know the loch like the back of our hands and it was not terribly difficult if you knew exactly where you were, and knew all your marks, which are known as transit lines, and the depths. We were in and out, night and day, and it was a responsible job and one had to be careful, but it wasn't very difficult even though it does sound as if it was somewhat tricky. The accident happened when the *City of Sydney*, a beautiful Australian ship on its maiden voyage, didn't follow my instructions to the letter as she had been advised to. The captain didn't let go the anchor when I told him to and he ran into another ship. He thought he knew better, and travelled on some way, and by the time he'd realised what was happening he had collided right down the side of another big merchant ship, thereby illustrating the enormously powerful momentum of a ship of that size. This huge ship slid down the other, and the big steel davits that carried its lifeboats collided and rolled up just like pieces of paper, with flames flashing with the friction and heat. He didn't let go, and he did an enormous amount of damage. But the captain was clearly at fault so there was no question of an investigation of any sort and we heard no more about it. I don't know what happened to him and we were too busy getting on with the job to ever find out, and I never troubled myself later on to find out. I'm quite sure that he wasn't flavour of the month with his company.

Of course, I have literally hundreds of memories of Loch Ewe, or HMS *Helicon* as the Base was called, genuinely hundreds. I was there for three years, working the whole time. I will mention a few more of the things that we did when I was there, but as you will appreciate I have very many other stories that I could tell.

One of the things about the job was that each time I changed ship I was always very fortunate in that I had good men and a good crew, and good petty officers. We weren't clever and we didn't think we were, but we worked hard and we were very fussy about detail and very meticulous in all ways. I was very pleased to receive a flimsy from the Captain of the base once, that said that whenever anybody visited my ship they commented that my crew seemed better than they could possibly have been. That pleased me a great deal because we never imagined for a moment that we were great seamen. We just tried.

We took Mrs Fraser Darling north to the Summer Isles once to see her husband for Christmas whilst he was living there. Professor Frank Fraser Darling was an extraordinary ecologist and conservationist who lived on the Summer Isles for three years during the war, entirely by himself, to test his theories by doing an ecological survey, and he wrote several books as a result. He lived off the land, and I believe that when we took his wife out to see him it was the only contact he had had with human beings during the whole three years.

On another occasion, I had to go around the base and visit the anti-aircraft batteries. I've forgotten entirely what my duty was, but as I went around, at one battery my shadow fell on some food that had just been delivered to soldiers from an Indian sect that were manning it, and because my shadow had fallen on their food they refused to eat it, and had to be re-supplied. I thought that was rather strange.

We had an incident when I hauled in cable at Loch Ewe and there was a torpedo caught up in it, but all we could see as it came up was the propeller end. It looked a pretty old torpedo to me but obviously we weren't sure, and so we didn't haul it right up out of the water but sent for the harbour salvage vessel which had derricks that could help us lift the torpedo up clear of the cable. Anyway, the salvage vessel came out to us and circled round and looked at it and said, 'Oh, I can't help you with that', and off he went and so I signalled the base. I can remember the exact signal I sent to the Duty Officer, and it was 'Send *Orb*'. *Orb* was a service vessel belonging to the base which was manned entirely by Norwegians, who were the sort of seamen that you only dreamt of being. They were all first-class, and had already forgotten far more than I would ever know. So, *Orb* came out and they got it untangled for us, and we got it ashore. Sure enough, it was a First World War torpedo that had been lying on the bottom ever since the First World War.

We had to do gunnery practice once, after the Captain (it was peaceful most of the time, and we had a quiet job really) of the base decided that our flotilla ought to have some gunnery practice with our somewhat ineffective armament. So out we went into the Minches and dropped a Dan buoy, which is a little buoy used for holding up the nets in fishing and has a pole of about ten feet stuck in the top of it, about two or three inches in diameter. This was the target. We fired at this thing from a distance of about a mile or half a mile away or something like that, and our gunner actually hit the pole. Now there must have been a great element of luck in that, but they gave me the shell case to that round and I kept it in my cabin. I brought that away from the Navy with me too, and Simon Mark has it somewhere, but on reflection I ought to have given it back to the gunner. He ought to have had it.

Another day, I got a signal to go and pick up a party of people from the mainland and to land them on Gruinard Island. It was an order, but I didn't like the look of the conditions as the weather was pretty bad. I was a relatively ignorant seaman so I asked my coxswain if he thought that we could get them off the shore and he looked at it and said, 'Yes sir, we can do it.' He was an excellent sailor, being a real fisherman, and we launched a boat and picked them up. The man in charge of the shore party had been worried. I discovered later on from the base wireless that they had been waiting on the shore, in disgusting weather, for about forty-eight hours, and that a civilian vessel that was meant to pick them up had declined to go in. Anyway, we landed them on Gruinard Island where we got called upon to help them a little and we discovered what they were up to. It was the island where they were making the anthrax bomb, and we had to help, but not with the scientific side of things. These anthrax tests were killing animals, and we had the unpleasant job of counting the corpses. We were sworn to secrecy at the time, however it's all public knowledge now and one can even go back onto the island. I have a letter from the Ministry of Defence from a number of years ago explaining to me what exactly happened, and how they cleared the island, and in the letter, it also says that they never did make the anthrax bomb. They didn't succeed. They made anthrax cattle cake instead and stock-piled it at Portland Down.

Another time I got a signal telling me to pick a few men as my ship was going to be out of action whilst we did a job. My men and I were to board a merchant ship in the Minches, called the SS *Albert Le Borgne*. You can see pictures of it on the internet. She was only about 4,000 tonnes, and she was a small tramp steamer. We were to send the crew ashore, and then we were to open our orders. Well, we boarded the SS *Albert Le Borgne* but then the master wouldn't leave his ship and we had to wait for an official from the Ministry of War Transport to come out and relieve him of his command, which delayed things by about twenty-four hours. When he had left I opened the envelope (this was good old 007 stuff), which carried instructions to go to a little loch just south of Ullapool. After we had arrived, several ships came out and moored us to a buoy, bow and stern, and at right angles to the shore and then they put big, chain curtains right round the ship. We still had no idea what we were there for, or what was to happen. It was completely secret and we hadn't a clue. Then I was called over to the flagship *Bonaventure*, and I was sitting in the wardroom when I recognised a voice behind me and it was Lol Stevenson, who I used to sit next to in grammar school. He said, 'You know what we're here for, don't you?' I said, 'No, we haven't any idea. I haven't asked any questions. We've been here nearly three days and we still don't know what's happening. I've been told it's all highly secret.' So, he said, 'Well, we're the Chariots.'

You may have heard of them, they were the human torpedoes and these trials were being conducted in utmost secrecy at the time. The theory was that two men rode a big torpedo silently up to an enemy ship, clamped the front cone of the torpedo (which held a bomb) onto the ship's hull and then scarpered, and then hopefully up went the ship. The drivers nicknamed their chariots 'gheeps'. Later they were tolerably successful in attacking a number of ships and became very good at it. They were followed by the two-man submarines. But these chaps were going to use the ship that I had brought in, the *Albert Le Borgne*, as a practice target. They had to try and get through the metal nets and get up to the ship without us spotting them. We had lookouts and we had to try and spot them coming in cutting through the wire, and getting to the ship. They had to try and get in without being caught of course. We were there for about eight weeks, and every evening on the quarterdeck of *Bonaventure* they held film shows, where the film was chosen by majority vote. The young men experimenting on the chariots always chose the same film whenever I was there:

Destry Rides Again. It is a Western with James Stewart and Marlene Dietrich, and the film was shown repeatedly with full audience participation!

It was very exhilarating work. Everyone was striving his utmost to beat the Italians, who had first experimented with this sort of small, two-man craft, and everybody was stretched to the limit. When a chariot came back and had to be hoisted on board they didn't pipe 'Lower deck' for crew to come up and man the falls, and pull on the ropes we had in those days, because the whole ship's company, everybody, even the ship's commander, would be on the ropes alongside each other pulling away. It was an exciting place to be. But don't get the idea that they were wild, woolly desperadoes, they weren't. That was the thing that struck me most. They were ordinarily quiet, thoughtful, hard-working and keen. They wanted to do the job and they were desperately anxious about getting on an actual operation. I remember a man in tears because he wasn't chosen to go after the Tirpitz. (You can read about that operation in a book called *Above Us the Waves*). He was a man called Matthews, and he was the same man who later on during the raid on Dieppe, went back to the shore and picked up Major Porteous and got him on his shoulders, back to the boat and away. He didn't even get a mention but Porteous got the Victoria Cross. Funnily enough, Matthews was the only man I ever met who quite openly admitted that he wanted to win some medals. He said that he wanted a DSO or a VC or something like that. He was a quiet fellow, and I don't know what happened to him. But there we are. We stayed on the SS

Albert Le Borgne for about eight weeks, as I say, where our duty was just sitting there and being vigilant, until in the end I presume they had no more use for us and we went back to Loch Ewe, back to our ship and back to our old duties. You can read about the Chariots, as there has been a lot written about them, and if you want to see them then the only two left in the world are at Eden Camp in Yorkshire. You can read there a lot of details about the trials and about the *Bonaventure* and all the people that worked there. It was an interesting time, very interesting, and it was nostalgic to go and see those two chariots in Eden Camp.

The PQ convoys were the convoys that went to Russia. If you go to Loch Ewe today you will hear a lot about how the purpose of its base, during the Second World War, was mainly to support the PQ convoys leaving from there and those coming back, or those that did get back. In actual fact, the PQ convoys were a very small proportion of the total work of the port, but they were very special. We saw them in and out and saw them away and waved goodbye to them, and in the Minches they were taken over by vessels that really could protect them. It was rather sad to see them go as one knew very well that a fair proportion of them wouldn't come back. One day I got a signal to go out to a ship and to pick up a Sub-Lieutenant Gradwell, arrest him and then to bring him ashore. So, we picked him up and I arrested him. He was quite gentlemanly about it, and in my cabin on the way back to base I asked him what he had done to deserve to be arrested. The Northern Patrol between Denmark and Greenland in the winter was a vicious job. They had to keep station whatever the weather and they went through hell. They sometimes went for days without any hot food at all, and when they came back into harbour sometimes the ships were damaged in the upper works due to the conditions. One of these patrol ships, the *Alouette*, would come in with the whole crew singing and miming as they came down into the loch: 'Alou-et-te, gen-tille Alou-et-te, Al-ou-et-te, je te plu-me-rai!' I can remember it as if it was yesterday.

Anyway Gradwell had got drunk on duty, thoroughly soused, and had done it on purpose to get out of being on the northern patrol. I thought that it was a rather odd thing to have done but he told me frankly, 'I've had enough of the work out there. I can't stand it any longer.' I thought that the next thing would be that he would be kicked out of the Navy or sent to the salt mines or something, but apparently, he got away with it and went back, because later on in the war he became a big hero on the PQ17 convoy. I know this because quite recently there was a programme on television about PQ17, a dreadful Russian convoy that lost many of its ships and Service ships. It was the worst convoy of them all, for loss of life, and out of thirty-five ships only something like eleven got back. It was terrible, but anyway the last third of this programme was devoted to a young RNVR Lieutenant Gradwell. It was the same man I had arrested a year or so earlier, but on PQ17 convoy he had been in command of an armed trawler and had shepherded three ships right up North into the pack ice and painted them white and then sidled them back down again, through the pack ice to Murmansk, and he was quite a hero. As I carried on watching this programme my eyes nearly popped out of my head, because after the war this same Lieutenant Gradwell became Justice Gradwell, the Judge who tried Christine Keeler in the Profumo affair, an infamous legal trial in 1963. I was very surprised to learn that the young officer I had arrested had become the stuff of legend, and had also got on so well in the legal profession!

Another time I was told to pick up a Russian Admiral, head of the Russian trade mission to Great Britain, to take him out to meet a Russian ship coming in with one of the PQ convoys. The Admiral came to see me after he had been aboard this Russian merchant ship and he told me, 'My wife is aboard that ship. I didn't know that she was aboard, but now she's here, could you kindly bring her ashore with me?' Well, I was a very insignificant junior officer and so naturally I said, 'Certainly, sir' to this great Admiral who was head of the Russian trade mission, and that I was glad to help. We brought her aboard and took her ashore with him. They were a charming couple and we had a drink on the way in and he said, 'When you come ashore, do come and see me', etcetera. We landed them and I didn't think any more about it until I got a signal the following day to report immediately to the naval officer in charge of the base. So, I sent for a boat, went ashore and went in to see the NOIC who wasn't at all pleased. He asked me in no uncertain terms what the devil I thought I'd been up to. 'What the hell do you think you're doing landing an alien with no papers?' I explained to him what had happened and he told me to get out, not very politely. What had happened was that the

Admiral's wife had been landed at the base, gone ashore but had then disappeared into the hinterland, thereby causing a diplomatic incident where the Cabinet had got involved. I thought that I was going to be at least hung, drawn and quartered, but I never heard anything more and was never in any further trouble for it. I don't suppose that the Russian Admiral lasted five minutes and was probably sent to Siberia. I have written to the Russian Embassy on a number of occasions, but have never received any acknowledgement of my letters. I asked that since I was the officer involved, could they tell me what happened to Admiral Polikoff and his wife. At this distance and time, you would think that they could tell me as it would almost certainly be in their records; but then, there are a lot of secrets still dormant from the war. However, recently Admiral Polikoff has appeared on the Russian Embassy web site as head of their trade mission at that time!!

A similar mystery surrounds an Engineers' base at Loch Ewe. This separate small base held about a dozen big huts with ten-foot-high wire around them and an Engineers' sign on the front gate, and it was situated near the cottage where Eileen lived with our son John. We saw the men going from shed to shed but they never came out. Later in life, fairly recently actually, I thought, 'What the dickens were they doing there? I'd like to know.' At this distance in time I thought that the authorities would easily tell me, so I wrote to the Royal Engineers and they told me that the base had never existed. Then I wrote to the War Office and they told me that the base had never existed. I then wrote to the Freedom of Information Office (of the Army, I think it was), and they told me that the base didn't exist now and had never existed. Finally, I wrote to the Whitehall Freedom of Information Office and they said that there was never anything there. In reply, I sent them a copy of a small booklet which a man had had published after the war about Poolewe in wartime, and there on his map this small base is marked. I added, 'This is the base I am referring to', and they replied, 'He must have made a mistake in making his map, because nothing has ever existed there.' So, your guess is obviously as good as mine, and I still don't know what all those men were doing there. But they were there for at least four years.

At other times, we were swinging at the buoy for two or three days without really doing anything. I recall the time when an aircraft carrier came into the loch and I received a signal to go to the captain of the carrier and explain to them that he needed to move as convoys were coming in and out. I was received in an extremely discourteous manner, with him saying that he hoped I'd break my neck, and he wasn't going to move and that he needed to stay there for at least four hours as he needed work on his engines. This attitude wasn't the norm however and when we were in the base off duty, visitors from the shore thought very highly of an invitation to come aboard for a meal or drinks. They thought this was special because the base itself was very minimal. Bare, wild country surrounded the camp of huts or sheds, after which there was nothing but miles and miles of countryside and mountains and nothing to do at all out of working hours. So, an invitation from us was highly prized in the base, and we had people fairly frequently aboard for a meal when we were off duty and in harbour. I remember once entertaining the Base Chaplain Clement Davis, who afterwards became Chaplain of the Fleet. He was a very good man and a good padre. He was easy-going and straightforward and he got on very well with all ranks. In the Mess ashore of an evening he would sit at the piano and play for people to sing, and even when they sang somewhat doubtful songs Clement would still keep going, bashing away at the piano. He was a fairly frequent visitor to my ships, and I recall one day saying to him, 'Do you want to stay to supper, Clement?' and he said, 'Well, it all depends on what you've got, John. And it also depends on what they're having ashore. Would you send them a signal for me and ask them what they've got for dinner?' He was always very direct. We laughed, and I sent the signal and received a reply at which he said, 'Well, I'll stay with you if you don't mind, but will you send them back the message 'Hebrews, 13:8?' Anyway, he stayed to supper with me and when he'd gone I looked up the verse in the Bible and it read something like, 'Jesus Christ: the same yesterday, today and forever'! But he was a very unusual padre.

On Loch Ewe, I remember that we had a reserve hospital ship and a reserve fleet oiler, and hidden away in a little loch called Tournaig off Loch Ewe we had a reserve ammunition ship, which was quite a sizeable ship full of ammunition. All of these vessels were stationed there permanently and their personnel never came ashore. We never met any of them. I suppose that they thought that they were better aboard than on the base in that godforsaken place. When I got ashore between bouts of duty I normally spent it at the cottage in Poolewe where Eileen lived with John, luckily. I was due for leave one time, but for a terrible bug that was going around the Base which meant that there was nobody capable of manning the Harbour Master's office, and so I was 'asked' if I would go there and run the office until someone was fit. Well, I didn't know much about running a Harbour Master's Office but I managed it and it wasn't all that difficult really. I stayed for a few days before I could go off to the cottage, and it was very interesting. I found myself making decisions and giving orders that I would never have dreamt of doing, but as with the piloting I'm quite sure that if some of the people receiving my instructions had known that they had come from a young stand-in RNVR officer they might not have carried them out. One thing about the job that I didn't like was having anything to do with the American liaison officer who was stationed nearby with a dozen or so men. He was purely liaison, and it transpired that he was the son of the owner of a great American Bank. The Lieutenant's office was only about a hundred yards from the quay, not much more anyway, but when he had to go down to the quay to take a launch out to an American ship, or to meet anybody, he called for his enormous American car and chauffeur to take him the hundred yards or so down to the quay. I didn't like this, and thought that he should have walked down. You have to remember that I had seen tankers torpedoed whilst attempting to bring petrol and oil to Britain, alight with flames from stem to stern, and to see this man wasting petrol in that fashion was terrible.

When I had been at Loch Ewe for nearly three years it became clear that our flotilla was no longer really required and that a number of vessels were being sent to other jobs. I knew that sooner or later I would have to go too, and then one day I had a signal to report with *Fairweather* to Surrey Docks in London. I had no idea what for, but we set sail and waved goodbye to Loch Ewe. Just as we were sailing out through the boom gate I had another signal to say that the Admiralty had at last granted us permission for a powerful searchlight to be fitted onto the bridge of the *Fairweather*, a request which I had put in two years previously. This would obviously have been extremely useful to us in the work that we had been doing. We laughed, and set off for London. This was towards the autumn of 1944. We had no idea in advance why we were being sent to London, of course. We made the trip and tied up in the docks between two enormous concrete structures, which it later became known were part of a jigsaw-puzzle-working Mulberry harbour. They were towering concrete structures and the word being put about at the time was that they were for the use of our invading forces as a sort of submersible fuel reservoir, which seemed a fairly reasonable assumption. Mulberry harbours were one of the single biggest enterprises of the whole war, I suppose. At first encounter, the Germans took three days to understand that what they were seeing was actually a working harbour, and later I found out that the chief designer was the Head of my son's firm, Oscar Faber.

Anyway, on arrival I reported to the base captain and was told that a flotilla of small vessels was being assembled to set sail for Hamburg, and that I was to be their senior officer. We had thought that the Germans would completely destroy Hamburg docks before they left, and we were to go in there to get the docks up and running again hopefully and prevent any further destruction. I was given the job of leading this flotilla, and what I'll freely admit I thought sounded like a daunting operation. It was not the sort of job which I had ever done before, and I frankly wasn't looking forward to it. I had to see that all the vessels were readied with torpedoes and anti-aircraft guns and smaller ones loaded onto huge landing ships. These were not landing craft but big landing ships that could take vessels of that sort. We knew that we would be going soon, and at last we got orders that we were to sail on the following tide. However, there was one big landing ship being loaded with smaller craft that the dockers couldn't get loaded in time, and I went to see the head docker who told me, 'We won't get it loaded for the tide unless we have overtime,' to which I said, 'Of course you can. You've only got three or four hours' work there at the most!' The tide wasn't until five or six hours later but he said that they couldn't do it, and so I said, 'Well, I've got a crane driver in my ship's company. I'll go back and get him and we'll get the job done,' and I set off back to the ship.

By the time I'd got back there was a message from the captain of the dockyard saying that I was to go and see him immediately. I walked into his office and his first words to me were, 'I hear you've been causing trouble among the dockers.'

131

I was very taken aback, and I said, 'No, I haven't,' and I explained to him what had happened. He turned his back on me and looked out of the window and said, 'Go back and sign their chitty immediately.' I started to say something and he said, 'I don't like this any more than you do, but I have instructions from the Cabinet that there is to be no trouble in the dockyards whatsoever. There's the second front to consider.' So, I said, 'Aye, aye, sir,' and I went out and signed the chit and the dockers had the small craft loaded in two hours and went home with three hours' overtime pay in their pockets. That type of thing took place throughout the war in the docks. I have thought about writing a book about it many times, and I am quite sure that it would have shocked people. If I'd done it years ago when people were still alive, any number of stories like that would have emerged once it was published, because I found that same attitude everywhere I went. It was my experience that the dockers kept to their pre-war demarcation limits and practices throughout the war, and I could give you half a dozen, unbelievable examples of this but I have never heard a word about it anywhere, or ever seen any sort of report or programme about it. In the end, as the tide on which we were about to sail was rising, the operation was cancelled at the very last minute. The Germans hadn't done as much damage to the port installations as we thought they had. I must admit that I was extremely relieved, but like everything else in wartime I suppose that one would have risen to the challenge when the time came.

I walked back to my ship after being updated on this latest turn of events, and mused upon what would happen next. The war was pretty well over in Europe, and I supposed that there was nothing much left for me to do here and that I would be on the list of men going to the East, which I didn't exactly relish. I was slowly strolling back to my ship when out from behind a big pile of timber stepped a man in a long, blue raincoat who called me over by name. It was dusk, and I was rather wary until I saw that he was in fact an Admiral. 'Shannon?' he asked. 'Yes, sir?' 'I've got a job for you,' he said. He told me to pick three thoroughly trustworthy men from my crew and then he explained what he wanted us to do and where he wanted us to go. He gave me a cover story and instructions on who I was to try and contact, and what help I could expect. It all sounded very complicated to me, but I said, 'How do we get there?' 'A landing craft will take you,' he said. 'They'll be expecting you, they won't know who you are and you are not to reveal your own identity or the names of your men. They're not to know anything about you except that they're dropping you in Belgium.' When he'd finished I asked, 'Will I get a signal, sir?' 'No, nothing,' he said, 'nothing is to be ever written about this anywhere or spoken about, ever; and when you come back you are to report to me personally at the Admiralty.' Well, I thought that this all sounded very strange and so I said, 'But I am not a member of the Intelligence Corps, sir, I've never had anything to do with them.' And he said, 'That's why I'm sending you. You're not known to anybody in the operations and there is a chance that you might find out what I want to know.'

I was naturally a bit taken aback by all this, but I did what he said. I picked three men and we went down to the landing ship, all in a hurry of course, and there was one there waiting for us. As he had said, they were expecting somebody although they didn't know who, and we boarded and the commander didn't enquire who we were or ask us anything. He turned out to be a crazy young RNVR lieutenant, because after we were aboard off he went and he immediately hit a ship fairly hard when exiting the dock. It was a bit foggy and he just went astern and set off down the river again; he didn't bother to signal or stop. He had rammed the ship and damaged its hull, and when we got to Tilbury he got a signal, 'Have you seen a landing craft with damage to its bows?' And he said to the signalman, 'Send back, 'No, certainly not',' just like that and on he went. I suppose he was the sort of man that you wanted in charge of a landing craft. Then we were going up the Scheldt and were getting astern of a convoy when we got a signal from the shore saying, 'Slow down, acoustic mines'. He said, 'Acoustic mines? I don't believe in 'em! There's no such thing; it's all German propaganda!' Well, we'd got about two hundred yards from the convoy when Whoosh! a ship was blown up just ahead of us. So anyway, then he slowed down and we carried on to Antwerp where he dropped us and I carried out what I was supposed to do. Over the years since then I have wondered many times about the whys and wherefores of what followed. We'd got Antwerp docks working again by then, and I had been

134

given a *laissez-faire* card that meant I could go anywhere I wanted in Antwerp. I could go anywhere I liked and see anybody I liked, and my daughter Eileen still has this card (it's a little moth-eaten now), and it is the only real evidence that I have of that journey. I did what I was told to do, and as far as I could tell I didn't learn anything of any particular importance. They transported us back somehow, in another landing craft I think, and when we got back my men went back to the ship and I went up to London and reported to the Admiralty. I was taken right down under the Admiralty, and taken an incredible distance underground until I was shown into a little office where one man was sitting behind a desk, and it was the Admiral. He debriefed me for an hour and a half I should imagine, asking me dozens of questions about what I did and who I had spoken to, and what happened when I had asked the questions that he had told me to ask, etcetera, etcetera. Then suddenly he sat bolt upright, banged his fist on his desk and said, 'Say that again.' It was a conversation that I'd had with a man I'd had to contact, and I repeated it and he thumped his desk again and said, 'Got him! Thank you very much. Got him! That'll be all, Shannon, thank you.'

Well, I've thought about it a great deal. I think that I was given a cover story that had no reality to it, and it was merely what I was to believe I was doing. What I was actually doing was making contact, and putting two and two together I think that the Admiral must have placed some information with a certain person in the Admiralty, and in my conversation with the man in Belgium something had been let slip. Something the man had said to me must have meant that he had this certain information too, and if he had that piece of information too then the chap in the Admiralty – the only man who supposedly knew the information – must have been a spy or a double agent or whatever. After the war I got a little gold bar to attach to my medals, which John has now, and on the back, it says, 'For Service in Germany', which is incorrect as I was in Belgium. It was a strange business from start to finish.

My men and I were told that the operation was privy to the Official Secrets Act and that our mouths were to be sealed on this subject for the rest of their lives. A postscript to this story occurred after the war when we were living in De Vere Gardens in Ilford. Two men in the habitual long, blue raincoats and Homberg hats knocked at the door and asked if they could come in and talk to me. I asked where were they from and they were from the Admiralty, they said. They asked me a lot of questions, in particular about one of the men whom I had chosen to go with me on the operation to Antwerp. Then they thanked me and said that would be all, and I said, 'Well, would you like to tell me what's happened and why you're here?' So, they told me that Charlie had been blowing his mouth off in a pub. That was eighteen months after the war.

When I got back from the Admiralty I went back to my ship to await further orders. There were no real duties left for my ship to carry out, and there were quite a number of other small vessels on the Thames that were being paid off at that time towards the end of 1945. I was next tasked with taking a few of these small ships back to Aberdeen. We set off up the east coast when of course, as luck would have it the weather turned bad and down came the fog. We were somewhere near Hartlepool I think when we could no longer really keep together because of the weather and as senior officer, I told the rest of the flotilla to proceed independently. I went on in *Fairweather*, and learnt subsequently that the other six or seven small craft had all decided to seek shelter and put into port to wait for the weather to improve. I was very anxious to get up to Aberdeen and I made a bad judgment. I decided that it was alright to go on, and to this day I am slightly concerned about it. I let emotion overcome my better judgment, when really the wisest thing to have done would have been to put in at Leith or somewhere, to wait for the weather to get better. I wanted to get to Aberdeen because my daughter Eileen was about to be born, and I wanted to ring up and find out how things were going and then hopefully get leave to get down to Devon. On we went up the east coast of Scotland between the mine fields and the shore, with me steering very carefully and constantly checking everything I could possibly check. We were proceeding somewhere north of Leith when I overheard the leading seaman say to the coxswain, 'I don't like the look of this do you, Cox?' And the coxswain said, 'Ah, it's alright, the old man's up top.' Now, the old man was me and the coxswain, who was an experienced sailor, was satisfied that everything was alright and that I had things under control. I was very grateful to him, and pleased too, because I wasn't a real sailor and I didn't know much about it when all was said and done.

All I ever did was to try and do my best, and I really had tried very hard to do everything properly for some years. I respected his knowledge of the sea, and to have a man of his experience say that he was happy that I was in charge gave me great personal satisfaction.

When we eventually got to Aberdeen we couldn't get into port, and as we had to wait until the following morning we hoisted an anchor light. The next day when I got ashore I discovered that my daughter had been born a few hours previously. I talked to the base commander and he said that he would pay the ship off for me which was very decent of him, and it meant that I could get away and go off on leave and meet my daughter, and I set off down to Exmouth taking with me the anchor light as a memento. It had been alight when Eileen my daughter was born, and she now has the copper and brass anchor light in her kitchen. I also took with me the chart I had used for that difficult journey, with all the details of our passage marked on it. Only a few years ago I lent the chart to a diving club in Aberdeen because it had a wreck marked on it that they wanted to get at, a wreck not marked on modern charts. Unfortunately, they cleaned the chart up in order to photocopy it, and cleaned off all my original pencil marks and notes. I have put back my rough passage on the chart, but unfortunately the original markings which I would have liked to have had on, are not there. But that's how it goes sometimes. Simon Mark has the chart now.

Eileen's christening was held in a local church. Before I had left Loch Ewe I had spoken to the base Excise man and told him that I would like to buy some champagne and he said, 'Do you want me to deal with this officially?' 'Yes, I want to pay the duty,' I said. He said, 'Do you really want to pay duty on champagne? Do you know what it is?!' He told me the amount but I said, 'I want to pay it. I want to make sure that nobody stops me and that it doesn't get confiscated.' 'Well, alright,' he said. So, he gave me the appropriate chits and it was sent on ahead. Anyway, when I got home I was expecting a glass of champagne to toast my daughter at her christening, only to find that they had had a party the night before and had drunk all the champagne and I didn't get any! Life can be hard.

It was the end of September 1945 and I was then home on leave, awaiting another appointment. The war in Europe was over and I discovered that I was very near to the top of the list to take a ship out to the East, and I didn't want that by any stretch of the imagination. A friend of mine, who was just above me on the list, had been appointed to command the Shah of Persia's yacht, which was incredibly luxurious and almost as big as a destroyer. I didn't know what he was going to do, but neither did he, and I was teetering on the brink of a job in the East when I got the offer of Class B release from the Navy. This was offered when one was needed in one's civilian working capacity. I had heard that I could leave the Navy on Class B release because I was a teacher, and that young teachers were desperately wanted. Male teachers especially were like gold dust. You could get a job anywhere in the country at the drop of the hat. Obviously there had been a shortage of young men in the profession for years, and all one had to do really was to find somewhere to live and one could get a job.

But before I could go, I had to have a medical and I was sent to see Surgeon Admiral Milne because of some trouble that I had been having with my back, who sent me off for x-rays and sundry other examinations, and then he saw me again and very kindly he said, 'Well, you've obviously got a bit of a problem there. I advise you to either have a manipulative operation or to wear your left heel a quarter of an inch higher than your right one for about two years.' So, I went back to see the Medical Board and they said, 'If the Admiral says that, he's the top man in the country at that sort of thing, you take his advice and try the heel solution first and don't let them muck around with your back.' So, I went off and had my left heel built up and it did the trick. The Admiral, kind chap, had also said, 'I think that you deserve a bit of leave, and I'm going to put your folder at the bottom of the pile.' That was sometime in October 1945, and off I went home on leave. I was still in the Navy and I was still on leave, but I had got the Class B Release Docket so I was pretty safe, and I suspected that I would have a few weeks' leave before they called me back and demobbed me. After a week or so I got in touch with the Admiralty and asked them when my release date was, and they said that it would arrive in due time, or words to that effect, and I went back to teaching, but I was still on the Admiralty's books until February 14 1946 when they finally released me. I had about three months' leave on full pay, and I had actually already been back at work teaching for a couple of months before they stopped paying me. I ended the war being paid by both the Admiralty and by Barking Education Authority which wasn't a bad way to finish.

Chapter Nine: Tigh-an-Uilt

At the beginning of July 1942, after John was born Eileen returned to *The Turret* in Hulham Road, in Exmouth, to live with my parents, but she found that straight away she wanted to bring John up by herself, and she found a room in a house nearby called *Windyridge*. *Windyridge* was occupied by a mother and her daughter and son-in-law, and they were very welcoming, friendly and helpful and Eileen found that there she could bring John up by herself. I was able to get home to see them when John was about five and a half weeks old, and whilst I was on leave John was christened by the Reverend Fullerton at Lympstone, which was the headquarters of the Marines, in an upturned ship's bell which is now in the Royal Marine Museum in Southsea. *A close association was maintained with my family home and my father delighted in pushing John in his pushchair on the rough roads in the vicinity. Of course, Eileen started immediately the difficulty of having limited resources. She managed this extremely well, this skill became a dominant feature of our lives together.*

They lived at *Windyridge* until John was about eighteen months' old. I had been working out of Loch Ewe for some time when it seemed that I might be able to get hold of a cottage to rent at Poolewe, about ten miles from the base. When I told Eileen of this possibility she immediately packed her bags and picking up John she set off for Scotland, where she rented a room at a house which was rather laughingly called the Poolewe Hotel.[38] It was just an ordinary house in the village where they took two or three guests, and where she waited in hope until the Laird agreed to let us rent a cottage called *Tigh-an-Uilt* (The Cottage on the Burn). It is now a fairly large hotel, and we have used it many times.

For me of course it was wonderful having Eileen and my son John there at the cottage. They lived there for nearly two years, only leaving Poolewe when our daughter Eileen was about to be born. Every ten days or so we came off patrol and came into base to get water, re-stock with provisions and re-fuel with oil. We were very democratic aboard ship and I would ask the Coxswain to consult with the men and ask them if they wanted to stay in the base, or to go down to Poolewe where the cottage was, and they always voted to go down to Poolewe. Saying that there was nothing for them on the base, it was just a collection of huts that people lived and worked in and there was absolutely nothing for them entertainment-wise at all apart from the occasional concert. Whereas if they went down to Poolewe they could take turns going ashore, and they made friends in the village, and I am sure that some of them made friends that lasted long after we left Poolewe. As to me, I could row ashore and go home.

When we first took it on the cottage was virtually a shed and was in a dreadful state. There was running water that came

---

[38] John notes that he did explain to Eileen the difficulties of doing this but she was adamant and had packed her bags and left before he made proper arrangements.

from a pipe that had been laid on the ground up from the loch and it came in through a wall in the kitchen with a tap on the end of it, but we were the only people in the village who had running water. *One normally found small fish in the water but we were assured that these tiny creatures were harmless and it was the things that one could not see that were harmful. However, my base passed the water as drinkable without boiling.* There was practically no furniture, and no real kitchen or utensils. I well remember that we had three saucepans, one with a hole in it, and only two or three items of cutlery with the odd knife and spoon, and a little crockery. As all the plaster was cracked and falling off we covered the walls with five or six layers of newspapers and thick flour paste, and then distempered it all over. We covered the kitchen in silver balloon fabric. We scraped the furniture, what there was of it, and varnished it. Eileen worked on the stove which was all clogged up until it became quite decent and shone. We had one fire to heat the whole house, an open fire onto which we threw wood and sometimes a little peat, and Eileen absolutely loved chopping up wood for the fire. The fire surround was a whitewashed slab, and every day she whitewashed this and re-lit the fire. We were able later to get some equipment from Dingwall, about thirty miles away. This was mostly second-hand pots and pans and kitchen stuff that Eileen could use, and we got some extra plates so that the friends who occasionally came through Poolewe were able to call at the cottage and have a meal. On the little time I got off, I frequently got home, and altogether it was a very happy time. It was a pretty tough time for Eileen of course but for me it was incredible, and Eileen gradually turned this shed into a charming little cottage with a garden and a big allotment behind. The cottage itself was quite near the gates of some famous gardens, called Inverewe Gardens, where tropical and sub-tropical plants were grown. The gardens were eventually given to the National Trust. I remember walking in them, as we were given the run of these beautiful gardens, and Eileen took John out in his chair there pretty well every day. Mrs Carson, an old friend of the Laird lived at the Lodge and she used to invite John over to play. She was a very wise old lady, and although I don't imagine that John remembers her she took to him quite a lot. The Laird at that time was a lady called Mrs Sawyer, but she had been born a Mackenzie. She used to give us fruit and vegetables, and flowers, so things weren't too bad. Although I remember the day when the Laird, the Mackenzie, said to Eileen, 'What was your maiden name?' 'It was Galbraith', said Eileen. The Laird looked down her nose at her and said, 'Oh, a lowlander', and I saw for the first time in my life what looking down your nose really meant. I believe that Eileen had declined to be her unpaid chauffeuse at the time; but on the whole, we got on pretty well with her and she was kind to give us produce. I didn't get on so well with her husband because he thought that I should bring him duty-free cigarettes and duty-free tobacco back from the ship, and I certainly wasn't going to do that. He said, 'Oh, you will, you will', but I certainly wasn't and I didn't get on with him very well after that.

145

It was a mile and a quarter from the cottage into the village, where there was one little shop where one could sometimes buy things, and Eileen used to take John in his little open pushchair (not like the modern ones) down to the shop. The shop was quite something, and functioned as the village pump. Poolewe village was a tiny village but people came in from miles around and a long way out into the hills to shop there. They would come in for the morning or I suspect for the day more or less, and there was always a crowd of women chattering in the shop. When it was time to milk his cow old Urquhart who owned the shop used to shush all the women out and lock up, and they stood outside or sat on the ground and went on with their gossiping until he came back from milking and opened up, whereupon they all trooped back in and carried on. And what could you get? Well, rations, insofar as they could get those sorted out in such a remote place. Remember, it was ninety miles to the nearest town, Inverness, and most of that was via a track with passing places. For meat there was only lamb, the Laird's lambs, and Urquhart would put a lump of lamb out on his counter and ask, 'A piece for baking or a piece for boiling?', and if it was for baking it came off one end, and if it was boiling you got the next bit from the other end! It was okay, though. There was one small farm, a sort of smallholding really, that was the Laird's Home Farm, and the farmer there would put swedes in a bag and surreptitiously place this over our wall after dark, because he didn't want the local people knowing that we ate swedes. When I had fourteen days' leave after *Aelda* was lost we worked non-stop on the house and garden, and the allotment. We gradually got the allotment going and grew green vegetables, which the locals didn't seem to grow. *Our allotment garden was excellent. We grew quite easily some of the best vegetables I have seen and yet the local people looked down on vegetable eaters. Cattle food they called in and Salading was 'women's food. Eileen had to become adept at using mutton because that was practically all there was but often fish was available including wild salmon which she fed to the cat.*

Poolewe was virtually cut off from the world. If one wanted to go to Inverness one had to get special permission, as you couldn't move out of the area more than twice in the year without special permission. Eileen took John up to Inverness to buy him some clothes only once whilst she was there, and we always remembered that he wouldn't wear the hat. He used to take the hat off and stamp on it until one day, perhaps six months after he had had this outfit, he went and got the hat and put it on, and he wore it forever after that. Eileen must have found life there very lonely, and she must have found looking after an eighteen-month-old child tough with little assistance and nobody to turn to. She had no medicines and there was no doctor, but in fact if there was anything serious she could call on the doctor and dentist at the base, and we did use the dentist and ask advice from the doctor. The doctor said, 'Don't drink the milk from the Laird's cattle because it's diseased', and so Eileen used powdered milk and the Laird was very upset when she found out that Eileen had put in an application for powdered milk. Eileen never knew when I was coming home until I arrived. The first she would know would be when the ship had actually anchored, and she would look out and see that we were in the bay and she then knew that at some point I would get home. Even when we had to anchor at the other side of the bay because the wind was fierce and blowing in a certain direction and it was nearly a two mile walk in the pouring rain to get home, it was a joy to do it. There were times when I didn't get home for a while and she never asked me where I'd been or what had happened. Once it was eight weeks when we were playing sitting duck for the 'Chariots' and when I arrived home she just said, 'Hello', and never asked me what I'd been doing. I wouldn't have been able to tell her anyway, except in general terms, and she accepted that this was how it had to be. I imagine that she started looking out to sea about ten days after my ship had last been in, to see if it was anchored there, but it wasn't, and then it still wasn't, and then it suddenly arrived back eight weeks' later. It must have been hard.

We fished a good deal in the loch, for excellent, mostly flat fish. Sometimes we spun for mackerel, but mostly it was flat fish, and they were very, very good indeed. We could also fish on the River Ewe as long as the Laird's husband wasn't coming home, but if he was coming home then the Ewe had to be kept clear for three weeks. At other times, half a bottle of whisky to the Baillie and one could fish in the river. Actually, I didn't fish the river but my friends gave fish to Eileen so frequently that she used to feed salmon to the cat. We used to dig up our fishing bait from Sandy Bay, near the entrance to the loch, which was near Auntie Jessie's house. Auntie Jessie was a remarkable lady who supplied us with eggs. We used to land near the head of the loch, where she lived in an almost forsaken little group of crofts. Auntie Jessie's was one of only three crofts that were inhabited, twenty-seven of them were empty, and she lived in a cottage all by herself until she was a hundred and one. I have some amazing stories of how the community helped Eileen after she moved there, which bring into focus the way that people lived together and the way they helped each other. They had to, they were a cut-off community, and it was quite normal for them to go out of their way to help each other. They thought nothing of it at all.

Ewe Island in the middle of the loch had three farms on it, and on a Sunday morning the women would row across from the island in a long boat (rather like a Viking long boat) that could carry about eight of them. They rowed across whatever the weather, and landed on the shore of the main land and went to the Kirk. They certainly did that every Sunday we were there. They were a very sincere and devout people, and on Sunday they always dressed up in their best clothes. They were very good people. One day the HMS *Devonshire* came into the loch and asked the local inhabitants if they would like to come aboard one Sunday morning and see a warship. Not that there were many inhabitants of course, very few in fact, but some of these came up and had a look around the ship and apparently thoroughly enjoyed it. They were shown over the *Devonshire* and given a coffee, and so forth. Well, the next Sunday the local minister preached a very fiery sermon against temptation, all about the hell and damnation coming to people who traipsed off on unscheduled pleasure visits on a Sunday. It was very poor farming land on the island, and I found it difficult to understand how they could eke out a living there. Living on the island they were subjected to all the bad weather that swept over the loch, straight in off the Atlantic. Conditions in the loch could be quite rough, due to the wind in particular, and as the wind channelled down into the gulley near Loch Ewe it became really, really rough with the water for miles around just one white sheet of steam, when there could be some very difficult conditions indeed.

There was another lady living locally called Mrs Stone who was married to a man stationed at the base, who called in at the shop one day for her rations. Rations weren't all that regular but they did arrive eventually, and Mrs Stone went to the shop, where she was told that there were no rations for her, as they had all been sold. So, she went up to see the Laird and told the Laird what had happened, and the Laird said, 'Well, leave it with me and come up tomorrow and I'll let you know.' Mrs Stone went up the following day and was told, 'You've offended the local inhabitants by taking recreation on a Sunday.' She remonstrated, 'No, I haven't.' Mrs Sawyer said, 'You were seen walking along the beach, for two or three hundred yards along the foreshore, on Sunday morning.' Anyway, Mrs Stone apologised and it was sorted out and she got her rations.

I don't think that I fully realised the problems that Eileen was having at the time. I was so taken up with my own happiness at being able to go home to her that I don't think that I really gave enough thought to the enormous problems that she must have had living there, and I probably didn't realise this until long after the war. *Tigh-an-Uilt* had very poor heating, and it only had paraffin lamps for light and no hot water system, and she was looking after a young child. There was of course no television but there were also no newspapers and she had no real company. She rarely left the cottage, apart from going into the village or walking round the gardens. She did get up to the base a couple of times by asking WRNS personnel down to look after John, so she came up to the base for a dinner where she was the guest of honour in the mess, and I remember once we attended a concert, but these were only two social occasions in eighteen months and she only once went to Inverness shopping.[39] But Eileen accepted that we were at war. Poolewe was not a place where she would normally have chosen to live, but she accepted things there. She even welcomed them and asked no questions, but it must have been very strange for her nonetheless. When we revisited *Tigh-an-Uilt*, as we did many times after the war, I often wondered what Eileen's memories

---

[39]John comments that when Eileen visited his base for a meal that he overheard a very tough leading seaman say to the coxswain, 'Cor, 'ave you seen the old man's old woman?' Once Eileen was prepared to leave her son, less than two years old, in the hands of the steward aboard ship whilst she accepted the base captain's invitation to join them for dinner. The dessert was named after her and the base captain remarked that he did not know that junior officers were allowed to have such elegant wives.

were because I spent little time with her after all. She must have had thousands of memories.

Well, whilst she was at *Tigh-an-Uilt* Eileen became pregnant again and it was decided in April 1945, at about seven months into the pregnancy, that it was time for her to return to my mother's in Exmouth. So, we packed and began the two-day journey back down to the South. It was quite a journey, with no heating in the trains and with a three-year-old boy to look after. When we eventually got back to Exmouth, John was sat on his chair waiting for his dinner, and then all at once he rested his head on the table, in his plate, and fell fast asleep. I suppose that he hadn't really slept properly for the whole of the journey, but we'd got there. We picked him up and put him to bed, and then I had to go back, straight away, back up to Scotland.

What did Eileen do? The very next day she went out, at seven months pregnant and with a three-year-old child by the hand and went around Exmouth knocking on doors to try and find someone who would rent her a room or a couple of rooms. Eventually, after a day and a half she found a Miss Walmsley who was prepared to take in an expectant Eileen and her three-year-old child into her charming house. She was a lovely lady, and Eileen rented a room from her and shared her kitchen and bathroom, and everything went smoothly. Our daughter Eileen was born in a small nursing home in Exmouth, which she was able to go and visit comparatively recently, when she was sixty or so.

Chapter Ten: Post-War

It is hard to describe in words our euphoria when the war ended, even if I was still on the Navy's books, but I remember that it was wonderful to be able to think 'I'll do that tomorrow' and to know that I was free to do as I liked for the first time in five and a half years. In Exmouth, with Eileen and the children, I looked around and decided that we would really have to go back to Barking. There were several reasons for this, but mainly I owed the Education Authority a debt of gratitude. When I was an ordinary sailor earning two shillings a day and later as an able seaman on three shillings a day, the Local Education Authority had made up my pay to what it would have been had I been a teacher. I had thought this was a very generous attitude on their part, although I believe that many Education Authorities did it. But I felt an allegiance, and furthermore the Education Authority promised me a job if I could find a house to live in. Barking was also one of three authorities in the country that paid the top rate. They paid the same as London County Council. Teachers were then paid at four different rates according to where they worked in the country, and Barking was a good, forward-looking authority that paid top rates and were generous to their staff. Barking also always appointed to senior posts from within their own area and so there was a good chance of promotion if one stayed with them. Barking is very different today.

So, I went up to Essex for a fortnight from Exmouth to find us somewhere to live. A lot of bombing had impacted on the

available housing stock around London and I spent my days
trying very hard to find us somewhere to live with no success,
until I was at the station on my way back to Exmouth when I
saw an advert for a bomb-damaged house in Ilford. I got my
bike back off the train and cycled over to Ilford and went and
had a look at it. It had been well-built in its day and didn't look
very badly damaged, and so I went to see the Estate Agent who
said, 'Well, I am the Surveyor for the area,' and he pulled a file
down from his shelf. 'This is the file for 43 De Vere Gardens
and it is among those that I am recommending to be repaired;
and they take my recommendations,' he added, and so for the
very reasonable sum of £845 I bought a fairly large, double-
fronted but slightly bomb-damaged Victorian house in Ilford.
The men got on with the repairs very quickly, and in the few
weeks we needed to make the arrangements to leave Exmouth
they were well on their way and had nearly finished putting
things right. There was still the odd hole in the wall, and they
did the final decorating and plastering and so forth after we
had moved in. We moved there with two, small children and
no furniture. We had nothing, like many other people, and it
was not particularly unusual after the war I imagine. We had
virtually no clothing. We had no money, and we had no savings
left. We had had enough left from the lump sum I had been
given on discharge to put down the deposit on the house, but
we had no other money. I don't know if you have any idea
what living in London was like at that time but we only had
electricity for two out of twenty-four hours. Soon after we
moved in it was winter, but we had no coal and we could only

register with a coal merchant after we had been in the district for six months. We just had to go to bed early and that's what we did. We all slept in one room on mattresses on the floor for about a year. We had no curtains, and so we cut branches from the trees at the bottom of the garden and put them up against the downstairs' windows. We borrowed bits and pieces from the family (and we were very lucky in that respect) until we could get together a few belongings of our own. We bought furniture as we could get it. It was utility furniture made by the Government, some of which is still in use today by the way.

We had only been in the house a few days when there was a knock on the door and a lady with three children was standing there who said that she was my tenant. I said, 'You can't be my tenant, I've bought the house.' Apparently, she had been a tenant at the house before the war. Everybody thought that she'd gone back to South Africa, but actually her husband had gone back to South Africa and she had moved somewhere to the North of England to relatives and now she'd come back to claim her tenancy. So, I checked it up and discovered that she had a legal right to come back, and that there was nothing that I could do about it. We talked about it and we agreed that she would take the upstairs and we would have the downstairs, and that she would pay me rent. She turned out to be a good tenant. She didn't pay a lot of rent, as it was controlled and I happen to remember that it was seventeen shillings and a penny, and she left it on the stairs on Friday evenings. She was a nice lady and we found that the arrangement worked perfectly well for the times and under those circumstances.

I had a job to go to of course, and in order to keep the wolf from the door I also taught evening classes for five nights a week for the first three months. We needed the money, but this meant that I had to cycle sixty-four miles every day across Ilford, Becontree and a bit of Dagenham. I cycled to work in the morning, came back for an hour or so at tea-time and cycled back to work, eventually coming back home at around ten or half past ten at night. I would put the bike in the passage way, tiptoe into our rooms, lie down on the mattress and fall sound asleep. This didn't go on for long of course, and I reckon that how Eileen was struggling during the day was far worse, but the war was over and we were together. We were doing what we wanted to and we were very happy. It really was a happy time in our lives.

Out of feelings of loyalty, I went back to Cambell School, the school I had left before the war, to at least offer them my help. I was back teaching Geography and no longer taught Physical Education. Geography had nominally really been my subject at college. As mentioned previously, there were practically no young men teaching anywhere in the country at that time and we were welcomed back with open arms. Young men had all gone off to the forces and their place had been mostly filled by married women, who would leave upon their return. In the same way, Eileen had to leave her job in the Civil Service on the day she got married. This ban applied to many women in those days who worked in banks, the civil service, the police, local authorities, teaching, and in many other jobs and professions: if a woman got married she relinquished her job, and this didn't change until sometime after the war. It's strange to look back on how society was back then.

In January 1946, in the middle of all this upheaval, Eileen's parents came back from India for the first time in eleven years, and they stayed with us in one of the downstairs rooms at 43 De Vere Gardens which meant that we didn't have a living room to use either. Eileen and I and the two children and Eileen's parents all shared the small kitchen scullery as our communal living area, but we just got on with things and at that time those conditions were normal. We were happy. We had had five and a half years of war and our cramped living arrangements didn't seem to matter by comparison. [40]

We were then suddenly incredibly lucky, and it came about like this. During the war, one of the vessels under my command had had some minor damage and had gone into a shipyard on the Thames to be repaired. The manager of the firm doing the repairs came from Essex and we got to talking, and in the course of our conversation I discovered that his brother was a builder. So, a few years later I thought of this and wrote to him, asking him for his brother's address, and then wrote to his brother, and lo-and-behold he had one licence with planning permission left from before the war to build a little group of small bungalows. These were out in Gosfield in North Essex, and we were fortunate enough to be sold the last one. It was

---

[40] To emphasise this John has written: THE WAR WAS OVER, we could accept anything, as ANYTHING was better than WAR. WE WERE TOGETHER AS A FAMILY.

only a tiny bungalow about eight metres square: that was the entire bungalow! But we decided that it would suit us, and we paid him £1,100 for this as well as a little extra land at the side to build a garage, which would allow us to run a car if we ever had one! The bungalow was made up of a living room, two bedrooms, a kitchen and a bathroom. Eileen's parents moved there with us so it was a little bit crowded at first, but we were very happy there, and by the time they came back three years later we had built a room onto the back and a detached garage, and things were comparatively easier.[41]

I declined an interview for the Headship of Cambell School, because I did not think that I had enough educational experience, but the County Education Authority had again said that if I found somewhere to live they would find me a suitable job nearby, and I was going to go to work in Colchester where there was a good job available as the Head of a Geography department. However, as we were moving into the bungalow the Education Authority said, 'We can't arrange this job for you until the beginning of next term. Would you mind helping out instead at Halstead at the junior school there for a few weeks as they're very short staffed?' I said, 'No, of course not.' My college had only trained secondary school teachers, and I was committed to secondary school teaching and had no thought of

---

[41] John writes that Eileen made it clear to him that she would be unhappy if he tried to place any barriers in the way of her parents living with them. Not because she enjoyed this but out of an inborn sense of duty. She felt that they had been forced to live in India and should not have their dreams of life here spoiled.

anything except going into secondary education, but I agreed to go to Trinity Junior School in Halstead to help out for a few weeks. To my utter surprise I'd only been there a few days when I came to the conclusion that teaching junior children was a much better life than teaching a crowd of secondary school children. It was a happy place and I liked it, so I wrote to the Local Authority and asked if I could stay there and they agreed, and they were quite content for me to stay there apparently.

I stayed on in the job, and then after I had been there a year I was asked by the Managers of the school (and also incidentally by the staff, which was rather pleasing), if I would stay on as Headmaster there. They were going to sack the incumbent because he wanted a second year away to continue on an exchange visit to America. Trinity was a small school with two hundred and fifty children, and Halstead was a small, provincial town but it was a very good place to live. I had been out of college some nine years by then but probably for six of those I had been in the Navy, and I thought that I needed more experience before I took on a headship. I was doubtful about taking on the role and so I consulted the Deputy Head, who had been acting as Headmistress. The Managers had told her that they would not be appointing her as Headmistress since the school was Church of England and she wasn't a member of the church, but she actually didn't want to carry on with the headship anyway. She came around to our house and asked me to take it on. She said that the devil you knew was far better than the devil you didn't know, and that she would happily be my Deputy Head as she knew that we worked well together. She was a lovely lady. Once when she went on holiday I found her car outside our house with a note on it saying that she was going away for a fortnight and that she would be delighted if we would make use of her car. We didn't have a car at the time.

To cut a long story short I took over the school. It was a splendid school, there is no doubt about it. It had a first-class staff, all considerably older than me and mostly fairly old-fashioned and set in their ways, but they were absolutely first-class teachers of young children. Just like the Deputy Head, they rallied round and made it clear that they would do anything they could to help me, and that they were pleased that I was staying. Well, under those circumstances one can't go wrong, can one? The school was in a very good catchment area, in a very staid, traditional area. You could look back through the school admissions book and see the same family names repeated every twenty-five years or so going back through generations. Parent-teacher relations were excellent, and to give you an idea of the respect in which they held the school, parents would get dressed up in their best clothes to come up and see me. I remember that one of the parents came and gave me the inkstand that had stood on Sir Frank Godbould Lee's desk. He became Head of the Civil Service, and was an old scholar. We had support from everybody: from the local church, from the local societies, from the shops and from the population as a whole. The school had been built in 1816 when the Church were the only people bothered about educating ordinary people. The buildings weren't great but everything else was absolutely top class. Discipline, which could be a huge problem in some schools in some areas, was never a problem at Trinity. There was never any question of truancy. The children came to school because their parents were sending them to _their_ school. They were proud of the school. There were never any absences, never any lateness. The parents always sent their children to school beautifully dressed, clean and tidy, and the children were polite and hardworking. The staff were the same, and it was perhaps altogether the happiest time of my long teaching career.

We had an unofficial Parent Teacher Association that didn't convene meetings except when something needed doing. For instance, we wanted to divide the hall in two so that the two classes taught in the hall could have a proper room each. It meant that we would have to do without a big hall, but the classes would each be able to have a classroom of their own. We held a meeting of parents and straight away we had all the volunteers we could want to put up a big dividing wall, and this huge project was undertaken. They also built a huge relief map of the district onto the wall. We then wanted to put some glass in the roof. The school was built a bit like a church, and was an old-fashioned school, with lofty ceilings and high, gothic windows that the children couldn't see out (which had points in its favour). We wanted to put glass skylights in the roof to increase the light, and we held a meeting and straight away there were parents who said that they could undertake the work. That was the sort of association it was. They improved the playground, and everybody just worked for the good of the school.

At the time, I used to cycle to school, and as it was only six miles away I could cycle home for lunch, and a hot lunch was ready for me on the table at twelve-thirty on the dot. We shared the bicycle on Sundays. We only had one bicycle between us because we didn't want to waste money buying another one, so Eileen cycled down to church at about eight o'clock, and I cycled down for the later service. We took part in a lot of the work of the village and the church, and in local events at Gosfield. Church affairs took up some time but not a great deal perhaps, and our church was in the village only a mile or two away from where we lived. It was a very small village and I became the secretary and treasurer of the PCC, and we got that more or less sorted whilst we lived there. I was also secretary of the Tennis Club, and voluntarily coached Halstead Town Football Club. The tennis club was only five minutes from our house.

I was a member of the Rotary Club and Eileen became a member of the Inner Wheel and took part in many charitable money-raising events. She also came into my school and voluntarily taught Elocution and did Speech Therapy. The Rotary Club was a very interesting operation. I was sponsored by the dentist and the doctor, with whom had I become very friendly, and I used to play the doctor at Squash every Friday evening, for about two years, even though I never won a match. He had been a Cambridge blue and was a very good player and took the greatest delight in hitting me with the hard, rubber ball. But I'd got a doctor to look after me so I was alright! We didn't have a car of course, but he used to pick me up, and after we had played he brought me home. That arrangement went on for most of the time we were there. I had become interested in coaching football and went and did the Football Association Coaching Course under Sir Walter Winterbottom at Loughborough University. He had been Head of the Physical Training at the Air Ministry and before that had been with the National Council of Physical and Recreational Training, under whose auspices the Play Leading course had been run, which I did before the war. Anyway, he was now the manager of the England Football Team. It was altogether a very happy, busy, fulfilling and interesting time in our lives, but Eileen's side of the equation must still have been very difficult.

When we moved into the bungalow in Gosfield it was very small but it was ours alone, and as with Tigh-an-Uilt, Eileen organised things again extremely well. We used the garden as an allotment for the four or five years that we were there and Eileen bottled and dried food (of course, we didn't have a freezer then). When they reached school age she took the children down to the village school and back. [42] She went to Halstead on the bus came back carrying the heavy bags of

---

[42] John advises that Eileen read beautifully to the children and of course taught them both to read and actually to write simply before they went to school.

shopping; but she didn't stop in the town to spend one and a half pence for a cup of tea because that would have been a waste of money, and she knew that she could have a cup of tea when she got home. All through this time Eileen made her own, and the children's clothes, and sewed bits and pieces for me, and our daughter remembers being between eight and ten years old before her mother was taken to buy herself her very first dress from a shop. Eileen also sewed all the household linen such as the curtains and cushion covers, and she liked doing it and made a very good job of it. It is very difficult to believe today but until John was about ten or eleven Eileen didn't buy <u>anything</u> specifically for herself. That is how we lived, but it was entirely due to Eileen's ability and willingness to live like this that we did so. We would agree to a household plan, and we kept to it. It meant that our modest income could be used incredibly beneficially and over the years we were able to buy reasonable homes, sufficient clothing and good food for the family. This was all made possible by good financial management. We also always managed to have a holiday of some sort, although these were very modest at first. We stayed in beach huts, and once in a chicken shed on a farm, and we went camping and then later still caravanning. For the camping holidays, when the children were small, Eileen had a book in which <u>every single item</u> we wanted for camping was written down, down to the last box of matches, and when these were all ticked off she knew that we were prepared for every eventuality.

John and Eileen with their children, late 1940s

Eileen's thrift meant that our children could always take part in any school-based activities they wished, and that money for school lunches and other things could be found. We were able to save the amounts of money that were required for the children to go to university and college, but only because Eileen was prepared to work as she did and to put away savings against those times. It is easy to forget that in those days, parents had to pay for their children's Higher Education. Certainly, I think that she was unusual in her economy. The well-being of the family in the future was always at the back of her mind at all times, and concerns for herself really didn't enter her mind. I remember things like changing the babies with non-disposable nappies, there were no non-iron clothes, there was starching and ironing, and even the towels and sheets were ironed, and no washing machine. Eileen never had a washing machine or a fridge until her daughter was a young teenager. I will perhaps tell you one story about how she approached things. We obviously couldn't afford great sums of money for electricity and gas for the cooking and heating, and we always wore a certain amount of clothes in the house but it didn't matter. Where we later lived in Romford, Eileen pinned up two graphs under the stairs and each morning after breakfast she looked at the meters, read them and put a dot on the graph which meant that she could see immediately if we were using more gas or electricity than we could honestly afford. If that was so, steps had to be taken to use less. Our expenditure was carefully controlled, but during this whole time we were happy, because we were moving towards certain goals that we had. They weren't very wonderful goals, in fact they were very simple really, but they were of our own making. We looked forward to our plans coming to fruition.

Trinity School's secretary was also the Lady of the Manor and lived in a big Elizabethan house, but she had wanted something to do, and she was a very good secretary. She didn't clock watch and would work as long as was necessary, and we kept in touch with her until she died. I also had four men on the staff (one had been a bomber pilot during the war) which, for a junior school, was very unusual. They all had abilities and were people of good character and so naturally the school did well and I will tell you about some of its successes. The County gave out four scholarships a year to public schools, and for two years running this little provincial school was awarded one of those four scholarships. The eleven plus exam was still in full swing, and the catchment area produced good ability on the whole, but Trinity School also punched far above its weight in obtaining places for grammar schools. Trinity won most of the local Football and Cricket cups in the district, and whether it was for the Football, Cricket, Rounders or Netball, they won it. We also had a few outstanding children at Athletics; it just happened that way. We won the North Essex Relay Cup in the Relay Competition one year, and the following year we won the whole County Athletics meeting. They put the cups in the Butcher's window and the local people paraded them up and down Halstead High Street, up and down the hill. Nothing like that had ever happened in Halstead before and the whole district was delighted. We were a bit hampered by the lack of facilities. We did do well at athletics, but the only training we could do was on the Vicar's lawn. It was a big lawn, but we could only really practice starting and going through the tape. There were a few children in each year who were outstanding when I was there, and had some of them gone on to schools where athletics was important I feel sure that they could have become international runners, but none of them did unfortunately. A number of the youngsters did go on to do great things in life and I have met some of them since. In fact, I met one of them quite recently. He is of course a man of about seventy now and will be at my 100th Birthday this year.

I remember in particular the children's bedtime when we lived in our little bungalow. There was a rush to get to bed at the right time because Eileen was going to read them a story. The children have probably forgotten it, but they would sit up in bed with their eyes popping out of their heads. Eileen read with all the skill of a gold medallist in elocution, a skill which she would never use again, not even when reading lessons in church, which I thought was a very sad waste of a great ability. At that time, obviously we didn't get out much together. We couldn't, but once my secretary invited us to a special occasion in Colchester, at a club she belonged to. Anyway, we decided that we would go and my parents came to the bungalow to look after the children. We got ourselves dressed up for the event and then went in to say goodnight to them. I can see them standing there now holding hands. John was about six I suppose and Eileen was about three, and their mother had got herself well dressed up for this affair and she looked very glamourous. She had on a beautiful gown of beautiful Indian silk and she wore a tiara, and they looked at her and a puzzled look came over their faces and then John said, 'You don't look like our Mum', and Eileen never got dressed up like that again. She would dress up, but never again did she really go to town and put the same effort into her appearance as she had that evening.

At this time, the tennis club was only five minutes from our house and we were able to play a great deal, the children would come around often and act as ball boy and girl. Often Eileen made a picnic which we could have at the club and some of my best memories of her are relaxing in a deckchair at the Gosfield Tennis Club. She worked of course for the village fete and I well

*remember when Lady Courtauld was going to open it. Young
Eileen, I suppose a little over two, was chosen to present the
bouquet. Her mother made her a complete outfit including a
cute hat, for the occasion. Daughter carried it off as if she did
this sort of thing every day, beaming on the guests after
divesting herself of the bouquet. I have to admit to watching
mother rather than daughter. I knew the anxiety she was not
showing.*

John and Eileen went to the local school and I think that on the
whole they had very happy lives there as children. Unhappily,
John was in the infants' school when three of the children in his
class contracted polio myelitis, including John. It was at that
time a dreadful disease. Only about nineteen percent of people
who caught polio were put into an iron lung in the hope of
recovery and only three percent of those came out with little
harm done. Many who came out of iron lungs and survived
were severely disabled. Lucklly, John was not one of them. He
suffered a very slight muscle problem as a result of the polio,
but not much else. We were allowed to go and see John in
hospital at Colchester, but we were only allowed to look in
through the window into the ward at the iron lung, and the iron
lung had a little glass aperture in it through which we could just
see his head. I can remember as if it was yesterday, standing
outside the hospital ward with his Mum and looking through
the window at John's head. I held Eileen's hand, and we stood
very close, and no word passed between us but at the end of
twenty minutes she looked at me and gave me a little brave
smile. I think John was in the iron lung for about three weeks,

but fortunately, with a little help from the hospital, he recovered fairly quickly. He did have to go back to the infants' school however, not to the junior school to which his class had moved. He had to stay in the infants' school for an extra six months I seem to remember. He was then catching up on himself all the way through junior school, but by the time he got to the end of the juniors he was able to pass the common entrance exam (the old scholarship exam) and he got a place at a good direct grant school in Brentwood.

After about five years at Gosfield we decided to move again because we wanted good secondary schools for John and Eileen, and there weren't any particularly outstanding secondary schools within reach of Halstead I thought, or none that could offer first class opportunities to youngsters. I also felt that I wanted to spread my wings a bit. The facilities at Trinity weren't really all that good. We made the best use of them, but the playground was small, the classrooms were poorly equipped and there was no central heating (there were coal fires in the rooms). There was also no proper staffroom as the staffroom was shared with the school secretary, and no Headmaster's room, not that I wanted one really, for a school of that size. So, I looked around and applied for the post of Headmaster at the Priory School in Romford.

Chapter Eleven: Romford

In 1952, I applied for and eventually obtained, the post of Headmaster at Priory Junior School in Romford, which was an unusual school in many respects. To start with it was a new building made entirely of aluminium, in an experimental design for the time that wasn't altogether successful. It was also a big school, and held up to nearly eight hundred junior children.

Priory School, Romford

We had a loudspeaker in every room which was used for school announcements and school radio lessons, and each child had a locker. The school kitchen could produce two thousand good meals at lunchtime, some of which were sent out to other schools. The kitchen was a big institutional kitchen modelled on one from the Ideal Home Exhibition, and the director of the kitchen was Mrs McKenzie, who was an absolute gem.

The school had excellent, large playing fields, and the biggest playground among similar schools in Essex. We also owned a lot of sports kit for a junior school and again developed a good sporting reputation.

I gathered together a top-class staff, and Priory had physical education teachers who were very committed to helping with the children's sporting activities.

There was competition to get onto a school team because the Football, Cricket, Netball and Rounders teams won the local championships almost as a matter of right.

Our staff often also ran the district teams, and were involved in the coaching of Football, Cricket and Athletics teams in the Romford district. We had a de-mountable Boxing ring and we also had an international trampoline on permanent loan, because one of the Great Britain trampoline team was on the staff. We also owned Badminton equipment for the staff to use, and a big hall where at lunchtimes and after school the staff could play Badminton.

We had a room set aside as a library, and run properly by one of the staff after school, when children were able to take books out on loan, and additional feature of the school curriculum that I haven't found elsewhere was that every day all the children did a short ten minutes of speech, verse and drama. The children were given a daily example of well-written text and elocution which they absorbed. When educationalists came into the school they quite frequently asked me, 'Where do your children come from? Have you got such a different catchment area from the other school in the next district?'

John, back right with netball and cricket teams at Priory School

Our children spoke differently from children at other schools in the district. It used to surprise people. Their manners were different, and people who came to the school noticed it. I know that when the children were at home, and outside school, they returned to their own vernacular, but their speech was different in school and I could see nothing wrong with that. They had a standard to which they could return. They would conduct themselves in a polite, mannerly fashion and they could speak properly, and I thought that that was worth achieving. This part of the curriculum came under the tutelage of my wonderful Deputy Head who also produced extraordinary plays for the school, which the children participated in for the parents to watch. The music teacher equally produced extraordinary concerts, and we had a stage and two Steinway pianos. We also had two marvellous choirs. The music teacher used to bring some of her orchestra to accompany the children, and sometimes some of her adult singers to sing with the children. Incidentally, the choirs did all their practising in the mornings before school. Later in life I went into three hundred schools around Bradford in my job training teachers there, and I never found a teacher who could produce choirs like those at Priory School. There was a competition between both boys and girls to get into the choirs, and getting into the choir was like getting into the football team. I remember once the local Director of Education stood up and informed the parents at the end of a concert, 'You have not been to a school concert, you have had the privilege of being present at a genuine musical occasion.'

We had a speech choir, which was quite unusual, and when we had concerts the speech choir always brought the house down. This came under the Deputy Head's remit too, and here again there was great competition to get into it. I haven't actually ever seen a speech choir in another school. There may have been others, but I never actually bumped into another speech choir in all of the rest of my career. Our country dance team had lovely, very distinctive dresses, which they were very proud of, which had been made by the parents under the direction of the Deputy Head, and of course they won the local dance festival. We had numerous clubs that were run by the staff. Every member of staff felt an unspoken duty, not forced upon them, to give something extra to the school. We had clubs for almost anything that children of that age could be interested in. We had an astronomy club with its own astral telescope. We had a dog training class, and we found parents who were able to come and help with this. We also had a kiln and ran pottery classes, and not many junior schools fired their own pottery. I had the notion that if any subject was being taught at school, in this instance pottery, I needed to know a little about it. I would go and do a Teacher's Course in that particular subject. In those days, there were Teachers' Courses by the hundreds. Of course, all teachers had to pay for both their transport and the cost of the Course, but teachers did go on courses frequently. We had all the Sports Clubs of course, and there was a religious club that was quite well attended. We had five lay readers on the staff, but none of them would take assembly as they said that that was my job. I once counted up that during my twelve years at Priory there were twenty-three clubs in total (not all run at the same time), which alone made it quite an unusual school.

Every week I tried to ensure that I taught in every class in the school, for however short a period. I insisted on going into every classroom myself and getting to know the children. Although it could be difficult, I managed to retain very good staff who helped each other and were friendly and committed to their work. Quite a few of these were genuinely outstanding teachers. In all the time I was there, out of all the staff there were only two who could not fit in with our ethos and I had to ask them to go. One of these was utterly useless and the other was extremely good, but he was a maverick and would not fit in with everybody else. He held a senior post, and I told him that he would have to give up the post if he wanted to stay or else he would have to go. I was worried about it at the time and thought long and hard about it. But in the end, I decided that the best thing to do was to take a deep breath and to say what I wanted to say clearly and firmly, in a friendly way. This I did and he decided to resign and to the chagrin of some of my staff he next got a headship and I suspect that he ran a very good school. But it was a very different type of school from ours.

Behind the school were hundreds of acres of open fields which we used for nature work. The school also undertook numerous visits. We were very keen on school visits, and occasionally the whole school went somewhere by train or by bus. So, I won't boast any longer, but it was a good school and the children did very well. I recall a time when I was concerned about something at school and I was talking about it at home and asking what I should do about it, and my daughter Eileen who was twelve or thirteen at the time said, 'Oh Dad, everybody knows that Priory is the best school in the district. You don't have to worry about that.'

As far as the work went we were very ordinary in our methods. We did not take any notice of the then current educational trend in do-it-yourself education. We believed that we were there to teach the children and we believed in teaching. We didn't give any credence to the idea that only the child knows how he can learn, or what he should learn. Consequently, we were at odds with the powers that be at the time most of the time. We were vehemently opposed to the movement that was spreading in education at that time, called freedom of expression, where everything had to be about creativity. Children were extolled as little creative genii who still couldn't read or write, and encouraged to think they were artistic at all costs. We were dead against that movement. I had to stand up to Advisors and Inspectors who were trying to spread this great vague freedom amongst schools because it patently didn't work. [43] It may have worked in the Malting House School with

---

[43] John has advised us that: 'He believed that much of the traditional teaching created a sound basis for education but he tried to widen the curriculum, with tremendous support from his staff. English and Social Arithmetic was taught and standards were pursued. He thought that progressive education was suspect except when taught by outstanding teachers. Much of the academic work was taught using traditional methods

three staff, three stenographers, fifteen children of university dons, and Susan Isaacs in charge, observing them and writing her books, but it didn't work in big schools like the Priory, where the children were carefully advised and had proper goals, and where they were streamed so that they could be guided to good effect. [44]

There were un-streamed schools all over the country after the war with fifty children in a class, and I thought that the pressure for schools to be un-streamed with children following their own 'bents' was a sort of lunacy. We didn't subscribe to it and the whole of my staff were behind the idea that we should have a much more controlled environment. *John would like to record that he had immense support from his staff at this time, who*

---

but the outstanding results from the rest of the teaching produced excellence in sports, music, drama, art, history, geography, science and community involvement. Every day every child had ten minutes elocution training.

'John still has great reservations about the manner in which education has changed. He knew R.A.B. (Rab) Butler, the architect of the 1944 Education Act and discussed it with him. John considers that the Plowden Report, which came later, may have damaged education all over the country.

[44]As described in the Foreword, it is assumed that John is referring to the practice of child-centred learning as opposed to the teacher-centred classroom. In the former children are encouraged to participate in active learning, in the latter teachers are the primary source for knowledge. Susan Isaacs 1885-1948 was a British psychologist and educationalist whose work spanned the first half of the twentieth century. She was a keen proponent of nursery education. Malting House School was a nursery school at which Isaacs worked for four years. The children came from generally well-heeled families. Some of Isaac's books were based on her experiences at Malting House.

did not all adhere to the full progressive education system but who did provide an outstanding diverse education experience for all the children at Priory School in the 1950s under his leadership with outstanding results.

In conclusion, the children loved coming to school. We had no trouble, as most schools did, and we had no trouble with absenteeism. Truancy didn't exist, and the parents supported us wholeheartedly. I could even give examples where parents tried to exert pressure upon us to control things more than we did. Direction and control did not make the Priory School an unhappy place, and it did not make it a difficult place to work in: it made it a good place for the children. They knew where they were and they knew how they could behave, and they had guidance as to what was good behaviour. They knew what effort was, and they knew that if they didn't put in the effort then it would be demanded of them. There was no 'do as you like' in the school. Perhaps with smaller classes, very small classes, more equipment and more money to spend, we may have relented a bit. But we didn't have much money to spend, we didn't have small classes, and we didn't have boundless amounts of equipment. We actually had to raise money via the School Fund for what nowadays would be regarded as quite ordinary things that should be supplied to a school. The items of equipment I have listed, such as the kiln, were obtained in this way.

At the Priory School, I again had a very good set of parents who supported the school a great deal. It was a busy life and my work could be demanding. Some problems could be educational for *me*, such as when I announced that all Jewish children could go into a separate room at Easter so as not to partake in School Assembly. The next morning there was a deputation of angry Jewish mothers waiting to see me at eight o'clock, very upset that I intended to treat their children differently from their friends. I tried to explain to them that I was trying to be courteous to their children, and to their religion, and didn't intend that their children should be treated differently from the rest of Priory children. Another time one of the fathers stormed up to the school bringing his wife with him in order to scratch the eyes out of a teacher, over some misunderstanding or other. He turned out to be a great friend of the school in the end, and I discovered that he had only learnt to read when he went to prison for the first time. When I asked him what he did for a living he said, 'I collect bad debts for bookmakers.' That was his work, and when I asked him, 'What qualifications do you have for that sort of work?' he looked at me, and said, 'Let's say I'm persuasive.' But he put his name in our book of parents who could do things for other parents if they were in difficulty, or needed assistance. If parents put themselves down in this register, they would state what they could offer. They might be able to mend shoes or cut hair, do stitching or tailoring, decorating or gardening. Then if I knew of a family in real trouble, through sickness very often, I would get in touch with the most suitable person to help and they would go around and do whatever it was that they had offered to do. Only I knew about it. I would get in touch with A and say, 'Can you go to B? The mother is ill and they could do with some cooking,' and it would all be done privately and quietly. When I asked the debt-collector if I could put his name down he said, 'I can't do anything, Mr Shannon, but I can supply a bit of money if you tell me anybody really needs it.' I thanked him very much, and there were occasions where he went around, anonymously at night, and stuck a little money through someone's letterbox.

It was a hectic time in our lives, as apart from the school we did activities with our children, and gardening and playing tennis, and I also carried on studying. I always believed in trying to keep up-to-date, and I've got a list of about forty teachers' short courses that I took and minor qualifications I achieved during my career. In time, I also took a couple of university diplomas and a degree. Life was incredibly busy and at times very tiring.

When we had decided that we wanted to move to an area where there were better secondary schools for the children I spent some time looking around the Romford area until I found a house called *White Heather*. Eileen hadn't seen it but she was quite happy, she said. I listed all its detractions but she said, 'No, that's okay, it's in the area that you want and it's big enough for what we want; it'll be fine.' It was actually a good house, but unfortunately it took us nine months to get the previous owner out. But at last he left and we loaded up our furniture, leaving behind our spotless little bungalow in an immaculate condition. We followed the furniture van to

Romford, and when we got there the furniture van was already outside the house but they still hadn't started to unload. The furniture man told me, 'Mr Shannon, this house isn't like the one you left, it's in rather a bad state.' We went in and it was in an appalling condition. It was good outside but it was like a pigsty inside. It was so terrible that Eileen wept. *I had never seen her in that state.* Anyway, we agreed to have all the furniture unloaded and put into one room, and then we started cleaning the house. It took a long time but eventually we got the house sorted out and got all the furniture moved to its proper place, and we lived there for twelve years whilst John and Eileen were in secondary school. It was a lovely house eventually. We turned an integral garage into a room and built a detached garage and workshop, and altogether we had a splendid time there.

The next time that Eileen's parents came home on leave they could be accommodated quite easily. They stayed with us for several months at a time when I was the headmaster at Priory School, but I cannot pretend that this didn't cause some problems. For the whole of the time that they lived with us, and this is including the time when they came home to retire, Eileen's mother and father never did a single thing to help in the house. They never set a table or did the washing up and her mother never, ever in the whole time that she was with us, made a cup of tea. Eileen even took her mother breakfast in bed. Eileen never uttered a single word of complaint, and she just accepted the situation. She worked hard all day whilst her mother didn't lift a finger. She didn't grumble, and she wouldn't allow me to deal with the matter. There were to be no bad thoughts from me. I think that she was afraid, actually, of doing anything to upset her parents, but it was an extraordinary situation. Eileen's mother once said to me, 'You don't count, you're only her husband. I'm her mother.' I wanted to say something but I wasn't allowed to. They were very nice people, but they were very difficult to have in the house and caused an enormous amount of trouble for Eileen, but she simply would not hear a word of criticism against them. Looking back on it, I have more sympathy with them. They did not overall have very good lives.

It was a fairly large house for one person to look after. The previous people had had help, a maid of work, but we couldn't afford that sort of thing and typically Eileen made a plan for the housework. Certain jobs were done on certain days, and in order that things be done right the routine had to be adhered to. I remember that on the landing upstairs we had two big Chinese chests that had to be polished on Tuesdays, and the Vicar used to do his rounds on a Tuesday and called in on that day. Usually he made himself a cup of tea and sat on the stairs to talk to Eileen for half an hour whilst she got on with waxing and polishing on the landing. Nothing was allowed to interrupt her routine but they could have a chat before he went. We lived outside town so the shopping had to be done by bus. Eileen took four shopping bags in and came back with all her shopping, and again she didn't stop to have a cup of tea in town as that was a waste of money. She also worked hard helping me with the garden, and in particular cutting the lawn was her pride. She used to endeavour to cut the lawn quicker than the man next door who had a motor mower and a similar sized lawn. We only had a push mower until I had to do it, when we got a motor mower. When I was the head of Priory I used to use seven shirts a week, all of which needed starched collars and cuffs, and there was the mass of other clothes that needed washing. We still had no washing machine or fridge, but Eileen had a very short spell in hospital to have a vein attended to, and the children and I were allotted different chores to do in the house. As it fell to me to do the washing I went out straight away and bought a cheap second-hand washing machine!!

Eileen and I always discussed it if there was any expenditure to be undertaken apart from very trifling things, and neither of us would spend money usually unless we had agreed it with the other. This was a matter of care because we had financial plans which we tried to stick to, but Eileen made all the important decisions about the children when they were young. It seemed to work that way, and I supported her in bringing up the children, and we never seemed to have a problem. I honestly cannot remember any problems with the children as they were growing up, and I have to say that this was entirely due to Eileen. The children went to good schools locally in Brentwood, but they gradually didn't need the same care that they had had when they were younger, and Eileen decided that she would now like to take up teaching and go to college and get qualified. She had done a little uncertificated teaching in schools near where we lived, and she quite clearly had a gift for it, because the head teachers had wanted her to stay. She applied to and got in to St. Gabriel's college where she negotiated with them to do a two-year course in a year. To do this she left home at about six o'clock in the morning and got back at about seven o'clock, five days a week. She did all her normal household duties as well including having her parents there for four months whilst she was at college. As an example of her positive attitude towards things, she would take the Circle Underground to college, which was about ten minutes one way or about forty minutes if it went the other way (it went in a complete circle). She took the long way around and used that time to read the literature she needed for the course and to make simple notes about the books she was reading. Our daughter Eileen has her mother's college record book now and I think that there are notes on about eighty-six books. She also has a vignette that her mother wrote on lawn-mowing for her English course: how she started pruning with the shears, progressing to a push mower until we got a motor mower, when of course we boys took over and she was back to fiddling with her shears again. It's rather a good little anecdote, or vignette really.

At about this time we bought a little Austin 8 car, when Eileen was thirty-nine. Then we had a Renault Dauphine which we sold after two years because I thought it was a dangerous car to drive. Even after two years I think that Eileen never actually knew that the engine was in the rear and not at the front; however, she was a very good tuner of engines and she helped me with the tuning and servicing work on our cars. We never allowed any garage to touch our cars, largely because we didn't want to spend the money on them, but also because very often they did not do a good enough job, and we worked on them with great care.

Whilst Eileen was at teacher training college the students were asked to put on a show of acrobatic dancing, made up of mainly modern dancing, and the lecturer got them into the gym to see what they could do. The six older students including Eileen stood at the side, and the younger ones were all asked to climb up the ropes to the ceiling, which none of them could do. Then the older members of the class were asked if any of them would like to have a try, and Eileen walked forwards and effortlessly climbed right up to the ceiling using only her arms. I understand that the rest of the class just stood around in utter disbelief. This meant of course that at the age of forty she became the leading lady in the dance routine but she wouldn't let me come up to see the show. I wanted to go, but she told me that I didn't; I explained to her that I did, but she told me that it would put her off, and so I didn't go. I would have loved to have seen it. She completed her teaching course and got a distinction in her advanced subject, and she immediately found a job at a school close to home, and then quickly became Deputy Head there.[45] She had a natural ability for the job and she was a very good organiser. This was a period of our lives when we worked very hard and things were going well.

---

[45]John has advised us that, Eileen's advanced subject was biology which enriched the rest of her life.

I was active in what we might call teacher politics, and I
eventually became the chairman of the National Union of
Teachers for the district and I also became the president of the
Head Teachers' Association, which kept me busy. Both were
interesting jobs, and it was interesting to learn about the
general background decision-making for education in the
district. I made contacts with other people in the same job and
had contact with the Education Authority officially, and
generally speaking I found it interesting. At one time in the
Romford area, the schools would shut down for three whole
days, each year, and all teaching staff had to attend a very big
teachers' symposium I suppose you could call it, instead of
going in to teach. I was the Deputy Chairman of the National
Union of Teachers at the time, and I had to organise the whole
thing. I had a great deal of help, of course, but I directed it.
There were probably about a hundred different teachers'
courses being run at different times of the day over a three-day
period. Some were short and some were long: some ran for
only an hour and were led by an expert who had come to tell
you about his pet project, and others covered the whole three
days and looked at an issue in depth. Usually a nationally-
known figure gave a half hour pep talk at the beginning, and
the year I ran it we had a well-known historian, who charged an
awful lot. He wanted money for accommodation as well as
transport, and in the event, he arrived a few minutes late,
straight off the train, and when he had finished talking he asked
if he could be paid in cash, and could somebody take him back
to the station immediately.

During this time, I also had a small but very interesting job sitting on the Borderline Committee for children who had taken the eleven plus exam. Under the Education Act there was a provision made for children to be transferred from secondary modern schools to grammar schools at the ages of thirteen and fifteen, although not many areas actually did it. Essex did however, and once a year we had to interview all the children who were borderline in the eleven plus exam, and then again, all those that were put up as borderline at thirteen and at fifteen by their schools. The job only lasted three or four days but they were quite long days. A small committee of us interviewed the children and we had the job of deciding whether they should change from a secondary modern school to a grammar school, or the reverse. As you can imagine it was a very difficult job and I resigned from it, saying that if I went home and had a bath and a sherry I would probably put a different name on the list, which was rather worrying. But the following year I was asked if I would do it again to keep the continuity, which I did as it had its interest.

It was a full life, but we did have long holidays. The holidays were as busy as term time but in a different way. Without those long holidays to relax and recharge and do other things, I think that any hard-working teacher would probably not last more than three or four years without having some form of breakdown. However, eventually the children went off to college, and perhaps life became rather humdrum. We worked very hard and we enjoyed that. We played tennis together a great deal, gardened a great deal and went to the theatre, but there was a sort of lull in our lives. So, I decided to take a sabbatical year from the Priory to go off to the Institute of Education at London University, which I found very, very interesting. I perhaps ought to say here that I was never honestly very academic. Looking back on it I probably used to look down a little bit on people who were purely academic but over the years I have taken several qualifications, merely because I wanted to keep up to date with some of the things that were going on. I took a Bachelor of Arts Degree in Social Psychology, a Diploma in Psychology and a Diploma in Child Development, and I have a number of yearly attendance certificates attached to universities, and have of course, as I said, been on a very large number of teaching courses. *I have never undertaken high level studies, but passing the Diploma of the Paris Chamber of commerce was difficult. Eileen and I took it together. The Diploma contains the complete fiction that we were able to undertake high level financial negotiations as a Frenchman (in French). I believe they passed us because we were old.*

During my sabbatical at the Institute of Education I spent the year studying for a certificate in Child Development with other educationalists and medics. I saw different types of education in action, visiting different sorts of educational systems all over the place and found that there was a very wide variety of education in Britain. At the end of that year I decided to do the diploma, so for the next year I worked very hard on a Diploma in Child Development and wrote a study which illustrated that life on council estates could be unsatisfactory for eleven-year-old children. Winnicott was perhaps our greatest Psychiatrist at the time I spent my year at the Institute for Education in London, and I actually do believe in Winnicott's ideas. [46] His theory is that everyone of us is made up of the influences upon us of every single person we have ever met, and every situation we have been in. He called it the theory of the generalised other: that every one of us is the product of everybody else's influence on us.

As a result of my studies I chaired a committee on the Worker and his Environment, a Local Government committee in the district. We took the Harold Hill area of Havering as the environment and we had a big committee of doctors, industrialists, psychologists and workers. We met regularly for about a year, and a doctor acted as our secretary and produced a very good report. The report was used by a government symposium held at Bristol, which was quite well known for a little while, and our report underpinned this. I don't know if it ever did any good, but at least it was interesting that the report was used.

Back at Priory School everything was running like clockwork, and there was less of a challenge. The staff all knew their jobs and worked well together, and I came to the conclusion that I was practically redundant. It was all running so well that after some years there were never any real problems, and when we had staff meetings we came to arrangements very easily. I had

---

[46] Donald Woods Winnicott 1896-1971

the good fortune to have a stable, dedicated staff who stayed in post, and in a sea of troubles I was very lucky to have them. Some of them stayed the whole twelve years I was there; they came when the school opened and they were there when I left twelve years later. The staff helped make the Priory School what it was. I had a truly outstanding Deputy Head whom the Education Authority did not wish to appoint initially because of her health record. They gave permission for her to be appointed on a trial basis for a year to see how her health held up, and when it did hold up she was appointed Deputy Head permanently. She was outstanding, and when later she became unwell again and tendered me her resignation, I said, 'I won't take it until you've seen another Consultant.' She went away and saw another consultant who said that she'd been treated wrongly and she was okay after that, returned to work and was hardly absent again. But when I left she wasn't given the Headship which I think she should have been. I was able to remain in contact with most of the staff after I left, but sadly most of them have now passed on, although I am still in touch with the children of some of those staff, and some of those children have told me about their children. They were represented at my ninetieth birthday celebration by a member of staff who was a natural trampolinist, and according to her colleague in the Great Britain Trampoline Team she could have also made the team if she had taken it up earlier. She was a Catholic and after she left us she had four red-headed boys. I reckon that she looked after them splendidly. She was at my 90th birthday, and intends to be at my 100th.

After twelve years in Romford, it was suggested to me that perhaps I might enjoy working in a Teacher Training College. We were both getting older and felt like a change and Eileen and I talked about it a great deal, and I decided that I would apply for Teacher Training. I got in touch with the Head of the Child Development Department at the Institute of Education and said that I was thinking about doing this, asking her advice, and she wrote back saying, 'Don't do it. You have a wonderfully creative school which is doing great work in the district. For goodness' sake, stay there. If you go to work in a Teacher Training College you will find it staffed by a lot of dried-up old spinsters with whom you won't get on, and whose attitude to education you will abhor.' I was quite taken aback by this reply and mulled it over, but then said to myself, 'If that's the case then I ought to see if the attitude of the College can change.' So, I applied to two colleges to teach Teacher Training: to Eastbourne which I knew as a town and as a very nice place to live, and to Bradford to the McMillan college which was quite well known in teaching circles. [47]

I got an interview for both colleges and I went off to the Bradford interview with an offer from Eastbourne in my pocket. The interview at Bradford lasted part of an evening and all the next day, and by about five o'clock the next day myself and another candidate who was being interviewed decided that we

---

[47] The college was named for Margaret McMillan who worked in deprived districts, notably Bradford. She advocated reforms to improve the health of young children, wrote books on nursery education and pioneered a play-centred approach to learning.

had had enough, and we informed them that we were going home and that they could send us the results of the interviews. A young man called Kerry Griffiths was the other candidate, and we went down to the station together and got on a train, and just as the train was about to leave the station a lady ran down the platform shouting out our names. We looked out of the window of the carriage and, huffing and puffing, she said that the Governors wanted to offer us both a post. I had already said that I would only go if I was appointed senior lecturer there, and yes, she said, they were offering me the post of senior lecturer and Kerry a post as lecturer, and would we go? We looked at each other, and with the train now moving we both nodded, 'Yes, okay, we'll come', and the die was cast.

In a sad sequel to this chapter, the Priory School in Romford was burnt to the ground three years after I left in an arson attack.[48] After it had happened I spoke to the local Chief Inspector of Police whom I knew quite well, and said to him, 'I'll give you the names of six children: it'll be one of those.' I gave him the names and he said, 'You're wrong. It wasn't one of them, it was two of them.' They were lads who unhappily had

---

[48] John has advised us that: 'Dycourts school, a completely independent school, was an identical building, built on the other side of the brick built kitchen which served not only to separate the schools but to provide meals for both schools. Dycourts school was not affected in the arson attack. After the arson attack, Pyrgo, a nearby infants' school where Eileen had been deputy head and designate head, was closed and amalgamated with Dycourts. The newly created school was named Pyrgo-Priory and taken over by The Drapers Company'. We are advised by John's daughter, Eileen, that in 2016, the SHANNON Year 6 block was added.

very tragic lives but I remember many children from the school who went on to have distinguished careers

Chapter Twelve: Yorkshire

In 1964, I had applied to the Margaret McMillan College of Education in Bradford because I had heard a couple of head teachers saying with a certain degree of pride, 'I've got a McMillan student coming in September', as if this was something special. I had discovered that they had always had a three-year course when most Education Colleges only had two-year teacher-training courses, and that their academic year started in January which was different from other colleges. When I was successful in getting the post in Bradford Eileen again said, 'If you can find us a house, I don't mind where it is.' I found a builder in Bradford who agreed to build us a house, but Eileen would have been quite happy with whatever I found. The house was in Baildon, and it was a splendid house and in quite a pleasant place, but unfortunately the builder went broke before he had finished it, and we had to finish it ourselves. The other problem we had was that according to my ordnance survey map there should have been a bridge across the river, but there wasn't, and so the twelve minutes that I had calculated it would take me to get to college turned into a thirty-seven-minute commute. I wasn't very pleased about this and the Ordnance Survey sent a representative down to pacify me who told me that they had made a mistake. They had printed a bridge on the ordnance survey map and it ought to have been removed, and I of course had relied on their map but having gone down to see that the bridge existed found that it didn't. Anyway, it was a good house, and the best small house

Raby's, the Estate Agents, had seen in twenty-five years when we came to sell it!

The college had about a thousand students by the time I left, all student teachers. I was appointed senior lecturer just as the college was changing fairly dramatically, although at interview they had not divulged quite how radically it was changing. It still came under the Institute of Education of Leeds University (one of the thirteen colleges that made up the Institute), but it was changing into a college that trained teachers for all ages rather than just junior school teachers. It was also going to have the Bachelor of Education Degree as its main qualification; and it had been a female-only college but it was going to become co-educational. I looked upon these changes as challenges until I got to know the college and how it was run, when it became quite clear to me that it was not the sort of place I wanted to be working in really. The thirteen colleges that made up the Institute had no exams whatsoever, and the degree work was all done by course work and there was no testing. For example, if a student wanted to join the Music Department she wasn't even allowed to play the piano for you to see if she could play, because that would have been an exam, or a test. You were meant to take their ability on trust.

After a year at the college I wanted to leave. The systems running at the college were to me incompatible with practically any form of good education. Out of courtesy I told the college that I was considering leaving, and then strangely a notice went up on the staff noticeboard to say that I had been appointed as

Principal Lecturer in charge of Professional Education, and Schools' Officer. At home, we were actually in a bit of a quandary because my parents had recently come to live near us. They were elderly and they had moved up from the South of England to live near us, and there was no question of them moving again. We tried to help my parents, and after my father died Eileen had my mother home to stay with us every weekend for years. When we had a caravan, she used to like to go to it. After work, each weekend we all went to the caravan and Grandma was very happy there. She wouldn't leave her own bungalow and eventually she died there, but Eileen cared for her a great deal. It turned out that being Schools' Officer was a bit of a challenge and quite a good post, and I was free to run affairs as I wished within the regulations of the university. I think, generally speaking I probably did a fairly good job, and I look back on it rather more kindly than I did at the time. I was also appointed Chairman of Assessors at the University of Leeds, and a member of their Board of Studies. But I was annoyed by the time wasted by university academia: the lunch breaks, the coffee and cake, the cucumber sandwiches, and the chatter, chatter all day long. A whole day would be spent discussing the simplest little thing, and then my colleagues were surprised that they hadn't been able to get through all the work they needed to. It was utter nonsense and I resigned from the Board of Studies as it really was a waste of my time. I was too busy.

When we moved to Baildon, Eileen left her own teaching job in Romford of course. She did come into Bradford to college to help when we were short-handed for a time, and they wanted to give her a full-time job but she didn't want it. Then I did some assessing in York College and they wanted somebody to work there for a term, owing to an illness I think, so Eileen went to work there as a lecturer and they wanted her to stay there as well. But she wanted to teach young children and wasn't at all interested in teaching adults. She then went to work in the village school in Baildon. The Deputy Head left soon after she arrived, and the School Governors immediately wanted her to take on the job, which she did. The infants' school where she worked was about two hundred yards across a busy road from the junior school, and so it was effectively run as a separate school. I don't remember being told that the Head Teacher ever entered it the whole time Eileen was there, and even though she was the Deputy Head, Eileen ran the infants' school, and of course it was a splendid school. I remember once when the Local Authority thought that she had been cheating on the reading standard tests that all schools had to do, because Baildon were so far ahead of other schools in the district, they sent in a couple of inspectors to check the children's reading and of course they found that a very high standard of work was being done there. Well, she enjoyed teaching. She also had a first-class staff who were all friends and who worked together happily. She never had the remotest idea what her salary was!!

I stayed in the post of Schools' Officer for eleven years and retired at the age of fifty-nine. I took redundancy when the college was merging with the Bradford Technical College and the Regional College of Art, in a bid to promote multi-cultural society. A political figure was being imported as principal of the whole combined college, and I didn't much like the idea, and in fact all the six most senior people retired at the same time. I came out at fifty-nine with a redundancy payment, on full pension, as if I had worked until the age of sixty-five, and I have never regretted it for one moment. On the actual day that I retired from the college I was offered a job as Head of the Postgraduate Department at York, but I turned it down. They got back in touch and said, 'You can do this job in only two days, but we will still pay you for the full week.' This offer might sound very attractive but I still turned it down. I knew myself, and I knew that I would work eight days a week if I started to do it. Their situation was that they had some good academics but they had had a very poor administrator as Head of the Department for a long time, and the Department was in an utter shambles. They needed someone for a couple of years to get the place running properly. It didn't need to be a top-class academic to do it, they wanted an administrator, and it would have been a good job but we wanted our retirement and I don't regret turning it down. Eileen retired at the end of the same year that I retired. She carried on until the end of the school year to see the children she knew finish that year, and I used to pick Eileen up from school after I had taken retirement. Once one of the children called out to her, 'Mrs Shannon, Mrs Shannon, your Daddy's come for you!', and once a little boy in my hearing asked her, 'Mrs Shannon, where do you sleep?' She was always there an hour before school started, and of course she was always there for a long time after it had finished for the day, so of course the little boy thought that she lived there.

When Eileen eventually retired there were tears from the staff, the children and the parents. Her Deputy asked if I could come and fetch her at a certain time on the day she was actually leaving, and as we were walking out of the school gates all the windows of the school were suddenly flung open by the children and staff, singing Eileen's favourite hymn.[49] It was quite a moving spectacle. I am still in touch with the staff who Eileen worked with at Baildon School, as well as the daughter of the caretaker. The caretaker has died, but he also found the school a lovely place to work in and his daughter has kept in touch with me. They all refer in glowing terms to Eileen, and she obviously impressed them. A member of the staff intends to be at my 100th birthday.

I also turned down an offer to be Principal of a small college in Newcastle after I retired. It was in the very early days of Information Technology but I didn't know anything about IT, and so I turned it down. They were going to pay me quite a lot of money but a friend of mine said, 'John, if they're paying you that money they'll want their pound of flesh. Are you prepared to give it?' I thought for a minute and I realised that I didn't want to work that hard any longer, and so I turned it down. I wanted time with my family and to carry on with our leisure activities and our holidays, and to work at home in the garden,

---

[49] John advises that Eileen's favourite hymn was 'Lord of the Dance'.

and all the other things we did as a family. I look back with satisfaction at the practical achievements of our family. Amongst some of the things we did over the years was to build three garages, a cabin cruiser, bungalow extensions, conservatories, a workshop, a coal shed, two car standings, and various patios. We had practically nothing done for us by workmen, and I wouldn't allow a garage to touch the car. We didn't have a car until I was more than forty and Eileen was thirty-nine, and after that we didn't allow work to be done on them by a garage until I was elderly, when car engines had changed to such a degree that one can't work on them as we did before. Eileen was a good engine tuner, and she even helped me change tyres on wheels, which people don't seem to do so much of today. At home, we never paid anybody to do the painting and decorating, inside or out, apart from one room we had done for Eileen's parents when they came to visit us on holiday, and that was done by Mr Kemp. He was a national champion rose-grower who lived locally, but he was also a painter and decorator and the room that he decorated for us was a work of art. Even the tiny parts where one might see a joint in the paper he coloured with pastels and fixative. The whole thing was beautiful. When I asked him about his job, he said that he was so completely inundated with work that he could actually pick and choose his customers, and when I thanked him for his work he told me, 'You put in the same effort for my grand-daughter.'

We did a great deal of work in the garden and a great deal of work on our huge allotment, which Eileen enjoyed very much until we saw a bungalow for sale one day when we were visiting our daughter in Birstwith. It was a good bungalow with a beautiful view and we bought it although its condition wasn't up to much. *It was in absolutely terrible condition but its position backing onto the River Nidd, with the mill weir in full view, was magnificent. It had a large garden on two levels.* We spent a fairly long time turning it into a reasonable home, but we never regretted it. Eileen settled in there very happily, she loved it and so did I, and we were able to have various members of the family over very frequently and it was altogether a good move.

Throughout our retirement we took many holidays. We enjoyed camping and caravanning, and staying in *chambres d'hôte*, as well as going on cheap package holidays. We had the children and grandchildren visit us at home quite a bit, and they seemed to enjoy coming to us. We visited Canada to see our daughter Eileen when she worked there. We had holidays in Spain, Majorca, Minorca, Tunisia, Italy, Malta, Scotland, Ireland, Belgium and Germany, and we had quite a love affair with France late in life. We had holidays with John, and quite a number of holidays with our daughter Eileen and her family, and they were always extremely enjoyable. We played a lot of tennis until I was seventy-five, and I would have gone on playing but some idiot at the hospital gave me an overdose of something or other and I wasn't very well for eighteen months.

Golden Wedding Celebration 1991

Through all my life until I got old I read a great deal. When we retired we went to many evening classes to learn all sorts of things: History, Geography, French, Latin, Italian, Spanish, Dancing and to Local History classes. Eileen joined in all of these and became proficient in Spanish and in French, and was a very good Old time and Sequence dancer. I wasn't much good but we went regularly and thoroughly enjoyed it. Eileen and I started taking a Diploma in French from the Paris Chamber of Commerce, which was fairly hard-going but we managed it, until towards the end of the course the Alzheimer's began to cause Eileen problems. She carried on with her evening classes and never complained about it, or spoke about it, but of course there came a time when she could no longer carry on.

Eileen was never ill during all the years that I knew her until Alzheimer's raised its ugly head. She had a few days when she needed a vein operation in Romford but she was otherwise never ill. She never had a headache. But when she was about seventy-eight the Alzheimer's disease began to take hold, and as it took hold she battled with it and never said a word about it to anyone. As time progressed we realised that she tended to follow me to get from one room to another. She couldn't walk down the corridor of a strange hotel and turn right into the dining room, for instance. Once when we were in Cyprus I needed to go into hospital, and I had to take her in with me, because she wouldn't have been able to carry on in the hotel by herself. Few people noticed it because she never spoke about her problems. She just got on with life and quietly walked behind me, or else followed somebody else. This situation went on for years, and during that time only the people very close to her knew that she had a problem. She sang in the church choir but for two or three years she had no idea how to find her place in a hymnal or the number of a hymn, and her friend found the hymn and then she just sang it, and no-one else knew. People didn't realise for some years that she had any problem at all. As a matter of fact, not even her close family knew for some years that she had a problem. She was a very private person.

As soon as we noticed a deterioration in memory power, literally years before it was even suspected by most people, we set to work to undertake activities which might help the situation. We went to see doctors, hospitals, consultants, psychologists, psychiatrists, and she was given medicine, and then she was given two hours of daily remedial mental work to do with me until one day she just looked at me and said, 'It's no good, John, I can't do it anymore.' She was exhausted and could not bring herself to try any longer, and I had to accept that. I can 'feel' that moment today.

She then went to a Day Centre in Ripon for two days a week, run by a lady named Rose with whom I am still in touch, and one day at the Day Centre she collapsed and I went to pick her up and bring her home. As I put her to bed our doctor said to me, 'You must face the fact that your wife will probably not last more than two or three days.' Well, she lasted for three more years. She lived on in bed for three years, but sadly, for one whose voice was important she lost the power of speech as well as the ability to swallow, so that for two and a half years she lived on a liquid diet and couldn't speak. Life is so unfair. We had carers for her, but even though she was bed-bound she never complained. One day I found one of the carers out in the corridor crying, really weeping, and I said, 'Whatever is the matter?' Through her tears she managed to tell me that Eileen had kissed her forearm when she had been helping her, because she could not say 'Thank you'.

On November 12th 2008, Susan, one of the Crossroads helpers had been looking at the newspaper and turning over the pages of the newspaper for Eileen to look at the pictures. We never understood at the time what she derived from this activity, but at least it was worth a try. Susan was patiently doing this when Eileen looked at the paper and suddenly, just quietly, she read a headline. The following evening when I was settling her down for the night she looked at me and she gave me the special smile that she kept for me, and during the night she passed away. The carer who had been with her a few hours earlier is still in touch with me today. Her carers were really quite devoted to her and some of them still come and see me. For the three years that Eileen was bed-bound, I was with her constantly of course, apart from a few days when I had a very minor stroke, when our daughter took over. For virtually three years I hardly had a day away from the house. When my wife died my life finished too in a sense, and there was a sadness and loss that I cannot begin to describe. I am not just saying it when I say that Eileen, or Mum, is rarely out of my thoughts, and at times in private I am frequently overcome to this day. [50]

---

[50] John has written that as he looks back he calls to mind that people used to refer to 'John and Eileen' as if they were one. He was told once that that was how they saw them. He never told Eileen but he kept a scrap of old letter, dealing with this matter, in his wallet. It's still there and rather 'over the top' refers to them as a 'golden couple'. He also writes that he never knew why she accepted him, when her choice in her home town was enormous but he has lived a life thankful for it.

Perhaps one last anecdote will illustrate our commitment to each other. From the time we got together after I left college I wrote Eileen a Christmas letter every year. It was a letter going over the past year a little, and looking forward to the next year, and the letters varied in length. When we were clearing up after she had died we found them all. She had kept all the letters. We decided to burn them with her when she was cremated, some of them in her hands, along with her wedding and engagement rings which were her only prized possessions. Eileen never gave any thought to the things we possessed, or placed any real value on any of our possessions. She loved her family; and she never grumbled or complained, whatever the circumstances. I cannot remember her ever uttering a word of criticism about any of her family, at any time, whatever they did, and I am sure that they sometimes deserved it. She was extremely self-reliant and she was never ill until Alzheimer's took hold some ten years before she died. It is a strange thing to say and I don't fully understand it now that she has left me, but having Eileen as a wife was far, far and away, the best thing that ever happened to me.

Dr Beer, our family doctor called the family together after she died and he said quite simply, 'I have practised medicine for thirty years and I have never seen a greater battle fought than your mother fought. I now have a new datum line in my practice for what can be done.'

I cannot begin to describe what an extraordinary person Eileen was. *Eileen was very attractive and very elegant;*

extraordinarily well spoken. Of course, she was intelligent beyond the norm and kind to a fault. She was very good at puzzles and crosswords. Eileen had a will of iron, when she wanted to use it; a capacity for enjoyment in small matters and a preparedness to take on any task whatsoever. Nothing daunted her and her quiet manner hid a reserve that was unsuspected. It is literally true that her weight, apart from periods of childbearing, differed by only 2 pounds or a kilo at any time. This was achieved by an effort of will, that was completely inborn. Friday evening, she would step on the scales. If her weight was up, she would have smaller portions of food. If it was down, she would allow herself a little of her favourites. This she was able to do with no apparent effort. I am sure of one thing that Eileen never had any idea of her own abilities.

We were together for seventy-three years until she died when she was very nearly ninety, and that is a long time. All who came into contact with her thought her exceptional. Two *patronnes* of different French *chambres d'hôte* where we stayed on holiday, wrote to me after her death to say that Eileen was the nicest guest they had ever had to stay. When asked to describe her mother to a large audience recently our daughter called her 'a real lady'. This is true, but she was a lady who was never happier than when she had a sledgehammer in her hand, or when she was mixing concrete, or digging heavy clay soil. She was exceptionally strong.

After Eileen's death, I lived for a while by myself. My son offered me rooms in Cambridge, in his house, but I took a flat in my daughter's house in Birstwith, where we had lived, and after that I moved into Hampden House, a big Care Home in Harrogate. I let *Stoneleigh*, our bungalow in Birstwith, but at the moment my grandson Simon Mark and his family currently live there, as they wait to move to France. They have taken back Eileen's grand piano so that for the moment it is back in the place where it belongs. It is a very good Care Home, and probably the best home in the district. The rooms, the staff and the food are all very good. It is warm in the winter and clean. Visitors can come at any time and they can even have meals in the home, but of course any sort of Care Home is a bit boring. It's a bit bare and most of the people in the house can't do very much for themselves, and so practically speaking I am alone in being able to get out and about. I am one of only two people out of the sixty-five residents who have a car, and recently I got a new three-year licence. I have a telephone and I have a television and books. I can also use an iPad. So far, I have been very self-sufficient. I order and arrange my own medicines. I have never had any real illness in my life, and in my working life I never took a day off due to illness, which I suppose is pretty unusual. When I arrived at the Care Home Dr Beer phoned me and said, 'Why don't you stay with our practice? We don't mind coming into Harrogate if you need us, we know each other, and perhaps it would be wise?' I thought this was very kind, and I took his advice.

Since Eileen's passing, I have become involved with a charity called *Carers Time Off*, as well as *Supporting the Elderly* and *Telephone Befriending*. None of these things are outstanding and I have not given a great deal of time to them, but it seems to have caught the imagination of some people, as I will explain. *Carers Time Off* approached me and asked me if they could put my name forward as Volunteer Carer of the Year for the district. I was quite embarrassed by this, but I came to the conclusion that some good would come of it, that they would get some publicity and that it may lead to more people volunteering, so I swallowed my embarrassment and agreed. There was some publicity surrounding the giving of this award of Regional Volunteer Oscar, which I won along with a rather hideous certificate and a rather nice clock from the Court Jewellers.[51] I was quite surprised, but I was more surprised still when I found out that because of this award I had been chosen to be one of the Queen's sixty Jubilee Champions. I thought that that would be the end of that, and that I could rest satisfied that something had been done to help the Association. But then I was informed that I was to be appointed one of the twelve Diamond Champions of the Royal Voluntary Service, and that the Duchess of Cornwall was going to give me a commemorative badge at Lancaster House.[52] John, my son, took me up to London where I received this diamond badge and yet another certificate, where Camilla also asked me to divulge the secret of my long life to her so that she could pass it

---

[51] In 2014, John was awarded the Harrogate Oscar for Volunteer of the Year.
[52] The Duchess of Cornwall is the President of the RVS.

on to Charles. I thought that things were finished then but no, the *Daily Express* ran a national competition for Volunteer of the Nation where people had to vote after reading your story. In due course, I found myself runner-up and there was some money for the society, a certificate naturally, and an iPad for me. But all this apparently did bring in more interest locally. *Carers Time Off* told me that they did get a certain amount of interest and even some more volunteers, so I was delighted about that. [53]

Early on in this garnering of awards I had been told that I was going to receive an invitation to a Royal Garden Party. People assumed that this was a corollary, or follow-on from the awards, and I couldn't find it in me to explain to everybody that it wasn't, because in a way it did happen as a consequence of being District Volunteer Carer of the Year. At that very first award ceremony, I had met the Lord Lieutenant's Deputy who had recognised my tie. We got speaking and he was interested in Belgium and I told him about the Royal Navy Section Belge. Well, he was extremely interested in all of this apparently and got onto the Lord Lieutenant of Yorkshire who arranged an

---

[53] John's daughter Eileen has advised us that in 2017, he decided to retire from *Carers Time Off*. He decided that he was getting too old to take on the responsibility any more. He continues to regularly keep in touch with the wife of one of his last clients and brings her to the local village luncheon club where he also meets up with the wife of another of his ex-clients. Although he is not actively working as a volunteer in the community, he has taken it upon himself to volunteer to visit and chat with 'room bound' residents in Hampden House. For some it is the only contact they have with the outside world.

invitation to the Royal Garden Party. Eileen, my daughter, took me and tells me that it was very good.

I have never done an enormous amount of voluntary work, but I have to give credit to my parents for starting me off thinking that a little voluntary work was a good idea.[54] Both my parents got gold 'Thank You' badges from the Scout movement, and I understand that these are quite rare. They both did voluntary work in the community, and I probably copied them. I have helped with youth clubs, and coached football at various levels from children up to semi-professional.[55]

I have taken part in many church activities, and visited the sick, the needy and the elderly. I have sat on church committees in different regions. I have been a Red Cross examiner up to cadet level, and examined badges for the Girl Guides. I was also chairman of the Girls' Nautical Training Corps at one time. My school encouraged voluntary work. Its motto was *Laborare et Servire* and I was the local secretary of the League of Nations'

---

[54] John's comments on his lifetime of volunteering can be summed up, 'If only everyone, especially retired people gave just a couple of hours, the world would be a much better place'.

[55] In 2017, John was nominated for an FA Respect Award without much expectation of success as there are many, many nominations for only 12 awards. The awards are given for service to football at grassroots level. On 21st July, the results were announced and John was the chosen recipient under the Supporter category. The award was presented by the Chairman of the FA in the Royal box at Wembley during the World Cup match against Slovakia on September 4th. John sat next to Stephanie Moore, the widow of the World Cup captain Bobby Moore whom John had known as a boy when he was a headmaster in Romford.

Union when I was seventeen. This habit carried on into college where I did Prison Visiting and helped at the Plymouth Brethren camps in my holidays, as well as visiting Casual Wards.

John, in September 2017 receiving his FA Award in the Supporter Category (See footnote n55)

King Alfred's College has grown into the University of Winchester, whose mission statement is 'To Educate and Serve the Public'. Our efforts at King Alfred's were recognised recently when the University of Winchester gave honorary degrees to all those people still alive who went through the teaching certificate course.[56] This ceremony was performed in Winchester Cathedral and Professor Joy Carter, the present Vice-Chancellor discussed with me how hard we worked and how much we achieved in just two years. Modern colleges and universities who train teachers do it differently now, and perhaps better, I don't know. But I give a thought to students today. Life of course is very different, I know, but perhaps some of the rigour that we underwent might help them. It might help them to have less disrupted lives and more satisfied lives, perhaps happier and calmer lives. Higher education now of course affects about fifty-three percent of the population and possibly quite a number of that percentage are not suited to academic work. I do not know whether it's good for our society in the long run to attempt to put more than half its number through higher education. I certainly felt some disquiet later in life when I became a lecturer myself in a more modern college of education, where my experience was that people no longer worked as hard as we had, and I thought that it was rather a pity. I found myself wondering again whether some of the discipline that we happily endured could not be well-used in some institutions today.

Winchester is a young university but it is improving year-on-year, and expanding already excellent facilities. Under their present Vice-Chancellor, they will I think become one of the

---

[56] The ceremonies were so well attended that there were both morning and afternoon ceremonies. John was invited to speak at the afternoon ceremony as a representative of the recipients. He spoke for exactly the time allotted to him, without notes recalling fondly his time at King Alfred's College.

best universities in the country. The University has increased its size, extended its student accommodation and hopes to have all eight thousand students living on campus in the near future.[57] A measure of the comradeship that existed between students at King Alfred's were the Winton Clubs for alumni of the college that existed in Manchester, London, Winchester and Portsmouth. I used to attend these at *The Cheshire Cheese* pub in Fleet Street. A benevolent society also existed to help any alumni who were in trouble or difficulty. The Winton Club of course is a dying club and gradually there will be no more people left who can call themselves Wintonians, but to date it still meets yearly for a reunion at the University and still hands out benevolent gifts where necessary to people who have fallen on hard times. My son took me to a Winton reunion a while ago where it was announced that Winchester's finances are in very good order, and that they have allegedly the best student accommodation in Europe. They also won a national advocacy competition and they regard themselves as the best law University in the country. I started talking to a cleaner at the reunion who was sweeping up and he said to me, 'Next year, sir, we shall be the number one law school in the country.' *We* shall be. He was a cleaner, and that is the sort of feeling that I hope is spreading throughout the whole of the University. Why shouldn't it be one of the best in the country? It has just been granted the money to double in size. I was honoured last

---

[57] John recognises that he might have the rate of increase wrong but he has the highest regard for the University's progress and wishes some of his colleagues could be around. Instead he tells their children.

year to be made an Honorary Fellow of Winchester University, and to lay a wreath in the Chapel on Remembrance Day.[58]

I am aware that I have left out too much for this to be a complete memoir of my life. This is really only a brief outline. You cannot compress a life, especially a life as long and as busy as mine has been, into a few pages or a few minutes. But I have enjoyed life and I have always had good friends. All through my life I have been fortunate enough to meet good people and I have kept in touch with people from all stages of my career. Nearly all of my contemporaries have of course gone now. I have no College friends left. I have no friends left from the Navy. I have no close friends left from teaching, but I am still fortunate in being in touch with some of the children and the students whom I taught, and some of the teachers that I worked with, and for that I am very grateful. I don't claim to understand life. I don't know what the future holds for me. I do know that I have been luckier than most people, and that I could not have asked for much more.

When recording these memoirs, I have been reminded of the help, kindness and the friendship that I have had, first from my family and then from everybody else. In particular, I am very aware of the many people who do not appear in this rushed work. I remember them all with gratitude.

---

[58] John was awarded an Honorary Fellowship of the University of Winchester at the graduation ceremony in Winchester Cathedral on 16th October 2014.